FROM PAIN TO PURPOSE

A Mother's Journey Through Grief and Love

VICKI REID

From Pain to Purpose
© 2026 Vicki Reid
All rights reserved.

No part of this book may be reproduced, distributed, or transmitted in any form or by any means, including photocopying, recording, or other electronic or mechanical methods, without the prior written permission of the author, except in the case of brief quotations used in reviews, articles, or critical writings.

For permission requests, please contact:
Little Brown Bird
www.littlebrownbird.com.au

Cover Photographs: © Peter Fogarty Photography (Front) © Vicki Reid (Back)
Cover & Interior Design, Editing: Sarah Lemcke @ All in the Edit

First Edition – 2026
Printed in Australia
ISBN (Paperback): 978-1-7642881-1-8
ISBN (Ebook): 978-1-7642881-2-5

*When I look up,
I don't just see clouds – I see love.
I see memories.
Do you look at the sky?
I wonder who you see.*

— Vicki Reid

"Do You Look at the Sky?"

In loving memory of Cooper

My beautiful son.
Forever 25.
Forever at the forefront of my mind.
Forever the most profound love my heart has ever known.

You were my firstborn—
the one who taught me how to be a mum.
At just twenty-five, we were still growing up together—
learning, laughing, stumbling, becoming.

Losing you broke me in ways I still cannot fully put into words.
The pain remains—real and raw—because the love remains too.

If there is any purpose in this heartbreak, let it be this:
that my story might help even one person feel less alone,
and that someone, somewhere, might know they are not lost in their grief.

This book is for you, Cooper—
and for every heart that has loved deeply…
and grieved just as deeply.

I love you and am so proud to call you my son.

And for Ashton—

For your strength, humour, and love.
For the way you remind me every single day that joy can still exist,
that laughter can still live in our home,
and that even through the darkest grief, we can keep finding light.

You are my anchor and my hope.
You carry your brother's love in your heart, and mine too.

Thank you for helping me keep breathing, for reminding me that
family still means *all of us*.

Note to Readers

This book contains raw and honest reflections on child loss and the lifelong journey of grief.

Some pages may be confronting. They speak openly about pain, love, and the moments that change us forever.

Please take care of yourself as you read.

Pause if it becomes too heavy. Step away when you need to. Come back only when you feel ready.

There is no right way to grieve, and no single way to read these words.

You may cry, you may smile, you may need to close the book and breathe for a while—that's all okay.

These pages were written with love, honesty, and hope.

I share them not to bring sadness, but to bring understanding—to remind you that even in the deepest heartbreak, you are not alone.

To every parent walking this path—you are not broken. You are love, carrying the weight of absence. I hope these words help you feel seen, even in the dark.

Symbolism of the Wave

Phillip Island became our happy place for many years.
On one of our first visits to the surf beach, a lady approached us and said, "Do you know your children are swimming in the rip?"

We had no idea.
It was at that moment we realised that if this was to be our home away from home, the boys needed to understand the ocean—to learn its power, its rhythm, and how to be safe within it.

That was the beginning of our decade-long connection with the Woolamai Beach Surf Life Saving Club.

Coop loved that club.
He became a lifesaver, completing his Bronze, Silver, and Gold Medallions. He volunteered on the beach and ran courses to teach others.
Ash joined Nippers as soon as he was old enough, and Deane and I volunteered throughout the years.

The wave represents both the island and the boys' love of the ocean.
It also represents grief.

At first, the waves are constant and overwhelming—relentless and powerful.
Over time, they begin to soften. They still come, but less often.

You learn to read the ocean the more time you spend with it.
You never conquer it—but you get better at riding the waves.

Contents

Prologue	1
Our Story	4
My New Story	7
Chapter 1: Oh My God, Cooper Died	9
Chapter 2: The Unbearable Beginning	16
Chapter 3: Choosing a Resting Place	19
Chapter 4: The Question That Breaks You	24
Chapter 5: Never Say At Least	29
Chapter 6: The Chair That Holds His Name	31
Chapter 7: Between Worlds	36
Chapter 8: The Ones Who Stay	39
Chapter 9: When The World Feels Too Loud	43
Chapter 10: The Day Compassion Went Missing	50
Chapter 11: Grief and the Glass of Wine	55
Chapter 12: Post-Traumatic Stress	58
Chapter 13: Why We Need to Say "Die"	61
Chapter 14: Supporting Someone in Grief	65
Chapter 15: The Stillness That Saved Me	71
Chapter 16: Where I Still Find You	78
Chapter 17: Spirit on Country	84
Chapter 18: The Price of Healing	89
Chapter 19: The Weight of Paperwork	98
Chapter 20: Through the Fog	104

Chapter 21: The Gift of Preparation	107
Chapter 22: The Forgotten Grief	110
Chapter 23: Sibling Grief	114
Chapter 24: Key Dates	117
Chapter 25: The Group No One Chooses	124
Chapter 26: The Auntie Heart	129
Chapter 27: A Love Lost Too Soon	132
Chapter 28: Men's Grief	140
Chapter 29: Grief, Marriage, and the Space Between Us	143
Chapter 30: Sleep, Surrender, and Small Awakenings	148
Chapter 31: What I Was, and What I've Become	153
Chapter 32: The Comfort of Fur and Faithful Eyes	157
Chapter 33: The Power of Love in Action	160
Chapter 34: Messages from Beyond	164
Chapter 35: The Messages Continue	167
Chapter 36: What Grief Taught Me	173
Chapter 37: Who Am I Now?	175
Chapter 38: Little Brown Bird	179
Chapter 39: Legacy: Love That Refuses to Disappear	182
Chapter 40: Until We Meet Again	187
Chapter 41: The Shape of Hope	190
Final Note: When the Words Stop	194

Prologue

I was comfortable writing a children's book—it's an audience I know so well after over thirty years in early childhood education.
I love reading stories. As a leader, my time in the classroom became less frequent, so when I went into classes to spend time with the children, I wanted to share something I loved. Stories were always my go-to.
I loved creating character voices, setting the scene, and drawing children into a world they could fall in love with. If I got to share one of my favourite books, it was bliss.

When I wasn't reading, I was singing. There was always a song in my head. My colleagues would often laugh as I broke into a tune that somehow matched the moment.

One of my absolute favourite songs to teach the children was *"This Little Piggy"*—in Jazz.
I'd teach the children how to make the jazz sounds—the clicks, the scats, the slides—along with the moves and rhythm.

A friend reminded me of that part of myself after reading *Do You Look at the Sky?* She asked me to teach her granddaughter how to "do the slide."
I had forgotten that part of me until she said it. It made me smile.

Writing this book, though, was never part of the plan. It began the night before my knee replacement surgery—not with a goal of writing a book, but simply a need to write. This story came to life between surgery, knee rehab, and physio. As you read, you'll see small references to those moments. When I came home, the laptop sat permanently on my knee—my constant companion.

I never thought about writing to heal, or to help others. When I started, I didn't think much at all—I just wrote. But then the obsession took hold. I couldn't put down the pencil or the journal, and when it moved to the computer, I couldn't get my hands off the keyboard. The words evolved so quickly in front of my eyes.

As I wrote, I thought about the pain.
The isolation.
The negative talk.
The way it feels when the world is on top of you, while you're already crumbling underneath.
As I wrote, tears streamed down my cheeks.

I also met the mother of Cooper's friend, Jameson, who had died two years before. That meeting made me realise the importance of connection with other grieving mums. I had seen this through my support groups, but this was different. It was a reminder that connection can be healing when it's grounded in understanding and compassion.

And so evolved the thought that maybe I could help others too.

Then, when I received clear messages from Coop, reminding me how I used to help others—and how who I was and who I've now become could meet in the middle—I realised something:
I could still be me, just a new version. One who helps others in grief.

And that's how *"From Pain to Purpose"* grew.

It snuck up quietly, then became my focus through both physical and emotional healing.

This book isn't a guide.
It's a window into one mother's love and loss.
If you've found it, I hope it sits beside you like a friend—not with answers, but with understanding.

If it brings you comfort, connection, or even a single moment of peace, then Cooper and I have done what we set out to do.
To show that love doesn't end—it simply changes shape.
That even through pain, there is purpose.
And that by sharing our stories, we keep those we love alive in every heart that hears their name.

Our Story

Our family story began in 1995, when Deane—my now husband—and I met in Loch Sport, Victoria.
We fell in love, and six weeks later we were living together. Eighteen months later, we were married.

We both knew we wanted children quickly. We each had strong connections with our families, and our parents were young when they had us—between 18 and 21. We grew up alongside them, and we wanted the same for our own children.

I had just turned 25 when Cooper came into the world on the 5th of December 1998. He arrived early, eager to make his mark—and that he did.

We were so happy. Our little family of three felt perfect.
Our precious baby boy.

Cooper, however, saw the world differently. He wanted a brother or sister. He asked constantly.
But we just weren't ready to change the way things were... Until 2005, when my nephew was born.

Holding that tiny baby in our arms changed everything. Our hearts expanded, and we knew we wanted another child of our own.

It took time, but in late 2005 we were surprised and overjoyed to discover we were pregnant with Ashton.

When he was born, our world felt complete.

Two beautiful boys.
Healthy. Happy. Independent.

We shared the best adventures through their childhood. So much of our life was spent at Phillip Island—endless memories woven into the sand and sea.

By 2024, everything felt perfect.

It was Australia Day weekend.
Deane and I were at Phillip Island, constantly on the phone with Cooper—now 25, living in Brisbane—and Ashton, 17, who was visiting his brother for the weekend.

It was Cooper's last weekend of freedom before his partner, Beth, moved up.

The phone calls were endless, full of laughter.
The boys were experiencing life together as bachelors for the first time—without Mum hovering, ready to do everything for them.

And then, on the morning of the 28th of January 2024...

Our world shattered.

Cooper died.

In that moment, life as we knew it ended.

We were forced to navigate grief—to somehow learn how to live again.

I'm still not sure how to do that.
But we try.
One breath at a time.

Because love doesn't end.

My New Story

My child died. That is my new story.

It is the story I never wanted, never chose, and never imagined could be real.
No dream, no aspiration, no plan ever included this. It is a reality I was completely unprepared for.

And yet, here I am.

I have always left my phone on during the night, in case Cooper needed me. I've done that since he first went out as a teenager, then driving, then moving out as an adult. Always wanting to be available for him. Always hoping he was safe. Always worried something might happen.

Now, when my phone pings, I wake thinking it's Coop…and then reality crashes back in, sharp and merciless. I lie there in the dark, wide awake, relearning the truth I can never escape. My child is gone. And I have to come to terms with that all over again.

Who I am now is shaped by this loss—by the space that grief has carved into my life.

I am still me, but I am also someone new—someone learning how to carry a love that cannot be contained, a heart that holds both joy and unimaginable sorrow.

I write because I need to build connection—with my child, with those who loved him, and with anyone who has walked this path of grief.
I write to say his name.
I write to make sense of a senseless world.
I write to hold my own heart together when it feels like it might shatter.

This is my new story.

It is painful. It is raw.
It is filled with a love that will never end.

And in these words, I hope that others may find understanding, solace, and a reminder that they are not alone.

Chapter 1
Oh My God, Cooper Died

28 January 2024 – Brisbane

Oh my God—Cooper died.

Cooper died.

What the fuck!

Ash was on the other end of the phone, telling me Cooper had gone. How did I know what he meant? Deane was standing in front of me, my whole body saying Ash was wrong. I was frozen, captured in a moment I can never take back.

He was wrong!
He said the paramedics were arriving.
They would save him.
Ash was wrong!

My body stayed frozen, like it was trying to protect me from what my mind couldn't process. I remember staring at nothing, unable to move, unable to breathe, as if I was suddenly made of stone and air at the same time.

I waited for someone to take it back.
For the phone to ring again with a correction.
For this to be a nightmare I could shake myself awake from.

There is no manual for the moment your child dies.

There is only instinct, disbelief, and a silent scream that has nowhere to go.

Then suddenly, movement. Panic. Noise.
The world forcing itself forward when I wanted it to stop.

It was the phone call that shattered us.

Next thing I knew, we were on a flight to Brisbane.

I don't even know how we drove home from Phillip Island, our holiday house—to drop off the animals, and to meet Deane's parents at our home in Beaconsfield, in the southeastern suburbs of Victoria.

Deane's parents drove us to the airport to get on a plane, to get to Ash!

From Melbourne to Brisbane is 1780 km—about 19 hours driving, only two hours to fly—but it was a long weekend, an hour just to get off Phillip Island, another hour home, another hour to the airport. Then the flight.

The pain, the heartache. It took hours to get to Brisbane. Hours to get to Ashton.

What the fuck!

Cooper died.

And Ashton's alone!

When we landed in Brisbane, we had no idea where we were going. A dear family friend—one of Coop's best mates, the same age, someone we'd known her whole life—met us there. We'd met her parents in antenatal class, all those years ago, and our lives had quickly intertwined. The family we got to choose.

She had reached Ash as fast as she could, about three hours after, and then came for us. She picked us up and took us back to her house. We were in shock.

On the next plane was one of our best mates, following us up. He'd asked when we called if he should come, and we'd said no. Thank God he didn't listen. How could we have navigated anything through our grief?

Coop had died.
Randomly.
Unexpectedly.
Our oldest son had died.
On the phone, laughing and talking to me the night before, and then—gone!

I learned a lot about strangers that day—how emotions strip away control. People can be so unaware. So rude. So insistent. They pushed to get off the plane first. I just needed to get to Ash. Normally, I'm patient—but not that day. When the captain said we'd have to exit from the rear, even though we were seated near the front to disembark first, I broke down, hysterical. Still, strangers showed no compassion.

Now, when people are rude or disconnected, I think differently. Maybe their child died. When a car speeds past, I think maybe they're racing to someone who's dying. Grief changes how you see everything.

Our friend organised a car, booked accommodation, ordered food—even when we didn't want to eat. He made us move. Function. When the three of us just wanted to crawl into a hole and never come out.

What. The. Fuck!

Cooper died.
How did this happen?

The next morning, my sister arrived. Leaving behind her grieving family to come and support us.
Now there were five of us—the two of them holding the three of us up, keeping us together, just holding on.

We went to Coop's townhouse. His home. His environment. Beautiful. Meticulous. Every coat hanger facing the same way, evenly spaced. Every shirt buttoned to the top, all facing left. Everything perfect.

My OCD (Obsessive Compulsive Disorder – self diagnosed) had rubbed off on him—eventually—it only took him moving out. I can tell you, as he grew up, there were plenty of screaming matches: "Clean your room! The hallway is not part of your room! Get your stuff out of the bathroom—Ashton needs to use it too!"
Normal family chaos.
And now, here we were. In his immaculate home.

Deane had never been there before. I'd been up to visit not long after Cooper moved in, to check he was okay, the fridge had food, and he was settling in. I am so grateful I did. Deane still talks about the feeling walking in—how much love filled that space. Cooper's home was made of love. Not death.

What the fuck!

Cooper died.

I don't know how we cleaned out his house the next day. I look back now and wonder—what were we thinking?
But we started.
We packed.

We waited until Beth and her family arrived so they could see the love Cooper had poured into that home, the life he'd built for them to start together. Living. Not dying.

What the fuck!

Cooper died.

We started deciding what to throw out, what to keep, what to send home, what to take. Thank heavens we thought about his clothes, the ones we would need to deliver to the funeral home—how did we even think about that?—We had no idea how we'd get everything home. We made rash decisions just to survive. Looking back, I think we knew we'd never come back to Brisbane again.

Cooper was in the morgue!
We didn't need to identify him—Ashton had already done that, at just 17 years old. The coroner's office advised us not to go—they said it was a horrible place.

My boy was in that horrible place.
The thought was unimaginable.
How could we survive this?
How could we survive a world without Coop?
So, we did the only thing that seemed logical: We packed.

We were blessed that my cousin connected with my sister and arranged to ship whatever we needed home. So many decisions made in shock. We didn't go back. We didn't recheck. We didn't rethink. When we told the townhouse manager we'd donate items to people who needed them, it dawned on Deane—Cooper had worked hard for those things. He'd earned them. Struggled for them. Lived alone. Paid his own bills. We couldn't just give them all away.
So we reframed.

We sent home what we could, so that Ashton and the nieces and nephews would one day have pieces of him in their own homes—honouring how hard he'd worked to build his life.

Ash and I packed the upstairs—his personal treasures, the things he'd kept from childhood. Cooper was sentimental. A hoarder of love. Cards from family, notes, sketches, Nerf guns (oh, how I used to find those bullets everywhere), gold from Sovereign Hill, sketchpads full of imagination.
Ash and I did this, while Deane and my sister worked downstairs.

We met Cooper's new friends—people he'd only known a short time, but who already loved him deeply. They were scheduled to go out that day with Cooper and Ash for mini golf. They arrived to an empty house, trying to piece together what had happened.

As soon as we met them, we could see the impression Coop had on them and on their little girl. They spoke of how she adored her new "Uncle Coop."

Cooper's boss said the same thing about his daughter. She talked endlessly about 'Oopper'. He would have been an amazing dad.

So we packed.
Broken.
Barely functioning.
Exhausted.
Unable to be together for long—each lost in our own grief.

We packed up Coop's life. The life he'd only just begun in Brisbane three months before.
We were blessed that my sister's company allowed us to store everything in their warehouse. We still visit and collect things—almost two years later, many boxes remain. The kindness of strangers through that process was extraordinary. What a gift.

When Ashton brings home a box, it takes all my strength to go through it. Sometimes I walk past it for months before I can open it.

Early on, I went to the warehouse to repack things into a smaller pile. Hours of sobbing. His childhood, teenage, and adult memories all in boxes. His life in boxes. And so was he.

What. The. Fuck!

Cooper. Died.

Breathe.

All Beth's things came back, too. She wore his clothes for months—both of us hoping maybe his smell would stay a little longer. It doesn't. Over time it fades. But when you catch it—his aftershave on a stranger—it hits you like lightning. You look around, hoping.

But Cooper died.
There were no more stories to be created.
No more time to hear his voice.
No more laughter about his childhood, the adventures of his youth.
No more career in Brisbane with a new and exciting chapter ahead.
No more future, no dreams of family, love, or happiness.
No more Cooper, living.

Cooper died.
And everything about that will always feel wrong.

Chapter 2
The Unbearable Beginning

Before the call, before the world shifted, there was just us—a family, ordinary and extraordinary in all the ways love makes life full. If I had known those everyday moments were the ones I would cling to, I would have held them longer, memorised them harder, breathed deeper in their presence.
We never think we are living a "before" story. We only learn that afterwards.

I can't start at the beginning. The pain is too hard. To think back hurts beyond belief.

My mind is fractured. Some memories are sharp, painfully vivid; others are fogged, unreachable, too brutal to touch. Pieces are missing—gone, shattered, buried somewhere my heart can't safely go. And yet I still feel them in my body, sitting low in my stomach, a weight that can never be lifted.

Those first days were numb and surreal. It wasn't shock—shock sounds temporary, like it passes. This was a collapse. A disbelief so total it felt like my mind refused to let reality in. There is no coming back from that moment. Time doesn't heal—it only makes the weight familiar. You will never get used to the loss. You just get used to carrying it.

It feels like a cliché to say, "I thought I knew what grief was." But clichés were written by people trying to survive something impossible. I've read that line thousands of times over the last 20 months and 8 days—614 days since Cooper left this world.

I know that when I read these words back later, I'll think: *How did more time pass?* Because that's the one constant—time keeps moving. The sun rises and sets. Over and over. It's repetitive. I don't know if those simple things will ever look beautiful again. They remind me that life goes on, even though for mums who've lost children, it feels like there is no life beyond the pain. The only reason we look at sunrises and sunsets is to search the horizon—hoping to find some presence of our child there.

That thought makes me think of the looks 'whole' people give when I say things like this. When I say *whole*, I mean those who haven't lost part of their soul. Even those close to me—to us, to Coop—still get to have reprieve. They get to be fully present in their lives. But for those of us who are broken, no longer whole, the pain and the heartache will always be here.

These 'whole' people look at you with disbelief—*How can you say such things?* I don't say them to shock or to be hurtful. I say them because that's my truth. But the look—you see it in their eyes before they quickly look away. That flicker of horror.

That same horror is written across my face every day, for the rest of my life without Coop.

I'll write more about how society looks at us mums like we're crazy. Maybe we are. Crazy with the love we now have to hold without anything in return. Crazy with grief, our hearts exploding. Crazy, finding a way to keep living without Cooper.

In those early days, everything blurred into one endless ache. Morning came, but it didn't feel like morning—just another stretch of hours to survive.

People spoke, the world moved, and yet I felt suspended, caught between what was and what would never be again.
I remember thinking, *How do I live inside this silence?*
How do I exist in a world that still spins when mine has stopped?

There were moments when I couldn't tell if I was breathing or just remembering how to.
Grief took everything familiar and rearranged it into something unrecognisable.

That's where the story truly begins—not with what happened, but with what was left behind.

Chapter 3
Choosing a Resting Place

How, in the thick of grief—when your world is crumbling—do you make such big decisions?

I Googled funeral homes. *Who does that?*

I was in Brisbane, alone on the balcony. Deane and Ash were inside—grief-stricken, trying to sleep—and in a moment of unbearable stillness, I searched. My fingers trembled. My heart refused to believe what I was doing.

I couldn't do it.
I rang my friend.
"I need you to do this for me," I said through tears. "I can't do it."

Deane and I had never even talked about what we wanted for ourselves in death. My family had always been cremated, so that made sense to me. Deane's family had always been buried, so that made sense to him.

But now, we were being asked to decide for our son.
That couldn't be right. Not for us. We were good people. Our boys were kind and caring—the type to cross the street to help someone. They volunteered, just as we did. So how was this happening? None of it made sense. It felt like I was trapped inside someone else's life.

My beloved friend stepped in and did the essential work—contacting funeral homes and cemeteries, finding out what was needed, what documents were required, how the process even worked. She was in disbelief too. None of us could comprehend that she was helping plan this for Cooper.

She supported us to make the right decisions. She arranged visits to cemeteries. Options were limited; most are full, meaning cremation is often the only practical choice. But after days of agonising questions, searching for signs from Coop—anything to guide us—we chose burial. We decided on the same cemetery where my grandparents rest.

We initially decided a few plots together, thinking the rest of the family would also make a choice to be with Cooper. But the truth is, how can anyone make rational decisions when they're lost in grief?

Eventually, Deane and I agreed on two plots, enough for a large monument—one day, we'd all be together there. And then came the next impossible decision: location of the plots in the cemetery.

Our friend came with us for support. She stayed close but gave us space—quietly stepping back while we argued about where the "right place" for Cooper was. It felt like choosing real estate, only this time for your child. There are no words for that kind of pain.

We found ourselves discussing things like paths, trees, sunlight, and access—the kind of details that would normally feel trivial. But when you're barely holding on, those decisions feel monumental. The pressure they put on your heart, your body, your relationship—it's indescribable. It's hard enough when saying goodbye to an elderly loved one. But for your child... it's unbearable.

In the end, we made the right choice. Though it was agonising, Cooper's resting place is peaceful and open—beside a wide path, easy to find, surrounded by space where children can play or family members can sit. There's room for a park bench, room to breathe.

You don't have to walk through the entire cemetery to reach him, and it's close enough for his grandparents to visit as they grow older.

It's beautiful, and yet, utterly devastating—a choice no parent should ever have to make.

The days that followed blurred together—endless paperwork, phone calls, decisions. I'd hoped to help plan his wedding one day in the near future, not his funeral.

The list felt endless:
The casket—wood, white or oak; inside satin, silk or natural fabric?
Flowers—roses, lilies or gerberas?
The colours, the photos, the video, the order of service.
The master of ceremonies—we wanted someone young who could hold a room, because there would be hundreds of people.
The music—oh, the songs—how do you choose the songs?
Donations, QR codes, registration lists, the gathering afterwards—morning tea, muffins or biscuits?
Pallbearers, cars, the hearse, the private burial, the wake, the food, the drinks, the tab.
Every turn brought another decision—each one so important, because it was the last thing we would ever do for Cooper. We had to get it right.

But how do you make decisions when you're numb?
We had to rely on others—something we'd never really done before. And that, too, was its own kind of surrender.

And then, the question no parent should ever have to ask—*How much does a funeral cost?*
How would we afford it?

We were lucky to have some savings set aside for life's "emergencies"—illness, an accident, a leaking roof. But this wasn't the emergency we had planned for. Nothing could have prepared us for this.

When you want to honour your child, money feels like the least important thing in the world. Yet the world does not pause.
Every choice—every flower, every song, every tiny detail—comes with a price. How can anyone measure the cost of goodbye?
And still, grief pushes you into decisions your heart is not built to make.

———

It took thirteen days from the moment Cooper died until the day we buried him. Thirteen days of red tape, paperwork, phone calls, and waiting—trying to bring our child home from another state, as though grief alone wasn't already impossible enough.

For nearly two weeks we lived inside decisions no parent should ever have to make. Every detail mattered, and every detail shattered us a little more. And then, when all the planning was done, when the day was done, there was only silence.

The knocks on the door slowed. Flowers stopped arriving. The meals, the visits, the messages—all began to fade. People gently returned to their lives, as they must. Meanwhile, we retreated into a quiet that felt unbearable. No Cooper. Day after day after day.

The world kept moving. The earth still turned, life still unfolded around us as though nothing had changed. But everything had changed. This was now our new normal, yet nothing about it felt normal.

So we learned to simply get up. Process. Breathe. Move. Exist. One minute at a time.
Trying to find a way to live—or at least survive—inside this new

reality.

And just when we thought we had survived the worst of the decisions, the next question came—the one that breaks you.

Chapter 4
The Question That Breaks You

The unexpected pain that sneaks up on you is constant.
It doesn't matter what day it is, or how you feel, or how strong you think you might be—BOOM—out of nowhere, you're in tears.

Of course, the unexpected triggers are everywhere. Songs, especially. (This is why I don't listen to the radio anymore.) I'd rather have the quiet thoughts in my head than songs reminding me of memories and sadness. Sadly, songs rarely trigger happy thoughts.

The pain I'm talking about is one of the reasons I avoid new social settings. It's the quiet questions:
Do you have children?
How many?
Do you have boys or girls?

I've trained myself to make it through those three. It's taken time, but I've rehearsed them, preparing for those moments. Ideally, I have a plan of exit before any more come.

It's the dreaded next question that always follows—*How old are they?* It happens over and over again. It's like a bullet flying through your heart.

What do you say? Ashton is 19. Cooper will forever be 25. He should have been turning 27 in December.

It happened in the patient transport vehicle from hospital to rehab for my knee. Small talk—always small talk—even when you try to close yourself off from it. Not to be rude, just to protect yourself.

And there I was again, in tears, as I said those dreaded words out loud:
"My son died."
Unexpectedly.
Tragically.
He died.

It happened again today—polite people wanting to connect, wanting to know more about my family—and once again, I found myself in tears, explaining that my 25-year-old son died.

Then there's the other question:
What do you do for work?
Why did you stop working?
What do you do now?
And again, the answer:
My son died.
The grief is debilitating. I was unable to return to work.

It never ceases to amaze me—the forwardness of people asking *how* he died.
I want to scream:
Do you want me to relive the trauma?
Are you so important that you deserve to know, when only moments ago you didn't even know I had a child?

Would we say to a childless person,
"Why don't you have children?"

Would we ask someone whose child is in jail,
"What did they do?"

Would we question someone who says their loved one is terminally ill, *"How long until they die?"*

So why do people think this question is okay?

In the back of that transport vehicle, I was fortunate to share a moment with the Patient Transport Officer who understood grief. She said she'd been nervous picking me up because of my surname, Reid. It was her late husband's name—he had only recently died. She showed me her tattoo, and I showed her mine—an infinity ring with Cooper's name and a native wattle bird soaring.

We talked about grief. When she delivered me to my room at the rehab centre, she hugged me tight. Her colleague looked puzzled—he had been driving and hadn't heard a word of our conversation.

Over time, I've learned to expect the pain and the tears that follow these kinds of questions. But the first time an outburst hit me in public—really hit me—was in a small clothing shop. My sister had arranged to meet me. There was no way I could have done it alone.

Deane had encouraged me to get a new dress for Christmas, and I'd agreed to visit one shop.

I was early and my sister was delayed. It was an extremely hot day, so I told her I'd be fine. I felt strong enough. I'd go in on my own.

Inside, I managed to get past the usual *How are you?* thanks to the number of customers in the store. I tried on some clothes, grateful for the distraction. The store was closing down, and there was a buzz of chatter between regular customers and the owner.

I quickly selected what I needed, eager to retreat to the safety of solitude.

As I was paying at the counter, the owner made small talk. She mentioned they were transporting stock to another store over the weekend, but her son had borrowed her car and blown up the engine. "Boys!" she laughed. "They drive you crazy—but what would we do without them?"

"What would we do without them?"

That was the question I'd been trying to survive.
How could I live without Cooper?
My mind screamed: *ABORT! ABORT! ABORT!*

I needed to get out of this shop and fast.

My body was shaking. My voice quivered. I got out of there as quickly as I could. My vision blurred. I made it to the car and burst into tears.

"How could we live without them?"
How could she ask that question, at that moment?

I had my psychologist appointment straight after. It wasn't the first time I'd walked into her office in tears. And it definitely wasn't the last—I still cry every single time. How do you ever stop crying when the person you love is gone?

Such a well-meaning conversation.
And yet, it made isolation and withdrawal feel like the only safe options.
I got the new dress—but at what cost?

The old me used to walk into a shop, make eye contact with the staff, and engage in conversation.

Now, when I'm brave enough to go—which is rare (a good way to save money on clothes shopping, I suppose)—my eyes stay on the ground. I hope they can see that I want to be invisible.

I used to think people who did this were rude.
Little did I know—maybe they were just surviving.
Maybe they, too, had something breaking inside them.

After moments like these, I retreat.
The world feels too sharp, too loud, too unaware of what it carries in its questions.
It's easier to be alone—safer—where I can control the noise and let the silence hold me instead.

But silence has its own weight.
It echoes with memories, with the things I wish I'd said, the moments I'll never have again.

Still, in that quiet, there's something sacred—a space where I can breathe, whisper Cooper's name, and let the tears fall without apology.

Maybe that's what survival looks like now—not moving on, but finding small corners of the world where I can simply *be*.

Chapter 5
Never Say At Least

I only know death as a phone call—the kind that ends your child's life in an instant.
No goodbye.
No chance to save them.
Just gone.

But I recognise the pain of other parents—the ones who sit by hospital beds, facing impossible decisions, having to turn off life support. A decision no parent should have to make.
Knowing their child will die and saying goodbye before they go.
It doesn't make it any easier. In some ways, it could be considered even harder. I hear these parents talk about the endless visitors, the pain of sharing their child's last moments, and then the finality of it all.

And then there are those who spend years inside the medical system—fighting for cures, being an advocate for their child, holding on to hope, trying to stay optimistic—until the day their child still dies.

For others, it's a knock at the door.

The truth is: it doesn't matter how it happens.

A child's death is the most devastating loss there is.

So please, never, ever say, *"Well, at least..."*

Because the only *at least* we want to scream is—
Well, at least it wasn't you.

Chapter 6
The Chair That Holds His Name

There is a hollow, painful realisation that comes with the weight of grief and the echo of what should have been—a realisation that some places hold your child long after you no longer can.

A chair—simple, physical, permanent—holding your son's name. Something that shouldn't exist yet now does. A reminder of a world you now have no choice but to navigate.

I received a call from the cemetery manager. The plaque for Cooper's chair was ready to be installed and they were inviting me to be involved.

I don't think anyone can truly understand how significant simple acts of kindness can be until they've walked this path. There's so little we can be involved in now that centres around our children. No more birthday cards to write, favourite meals to cook, no organising their engagement, wedding, baby showers for their children, their 30th, 40th, 50th—the list is endless.

So when I'm invited to be there for something, even the hanging of a plaque, it means the world.

～

My weekly ritual began once Cooper's monument was installed. Until then, seeing only the dirt on the grave, marked by a temporary cross, was simply too painful.

When the monument was finally erected, it was easier—not easy, but less confronting. It held *presence*—like Coop. It was impressive, solid, and strong. And although every time I visit, I imagine Coop in that box beneath the ground, the monument's beauty is less confronting than the dirt ever was.

So, each week I would visit, picnic rug and greenery in hand, ready to make his resting space perfect.

At some stage I decided to request permission to donate a park bench in his honour. The approval came through on my birthday—it felt like a gift from Coop.

It also meant that for his birthday, three days after mine, and for Christmas twenty days later, the whole family could contribute to a gift for Coop.

Just a few days before that, I had taken Coop off my Christmas list. It broke my heart. But as soon as I got the okay for the chair, I put him back on the list. That small act brought such relief. I realised that Coop would always need to be on the list—that there would always be something I can do for him. It was an important moment.

It took some time for the chair to be installed, but the cemetery team was amazing from the very beginning. I was invited to be there for the installation. They recognised the need for a 'crazy' mum to be involved.

My OCD wasn't a problem—it was embraced. They encouraged me to check the height, to use the tape measure, to make sure it was centred. So sweet.

The ultimate gift came when they said his name—*Cooper*. They said it without hesitation or fear, but with compassion.

They didn't think it was strange when I asked them not to poison the grass edges around the base. They encouraged me to grow seed, to buy a hose, to do whatever I needed to make it perfect.

Thanks to their kindness, I now have a trolley filled with tools to care for Coop's space: to water, mow, fertilise, trim, clean, arrange—and to write. This is where my children's books have been written.

Being invited to be there when the plaque was installed meant the world. It was a beautiful Saturday morning, the sun shining, our border collies bounding around us. Deane and I were there to assist—but really, just to be present.

Now everyone who sits on that chair knows it's Cooper's chair. They can see and feel the love that surrounds our beautiful boy.

It's not the big things that matter—it's the small gestures, the kindness, the love shown. When everyone else has gone, these small gestures become *monumental*.

I will always be grateful for these moments.

As I sit on Coop's chair and write, I know the people who work at the cemetery know his name—and that they care about the details. I know that Cooper matters.

This helps me feel comfortable in my rituals: cutting the grass with my trimmers, snipping the edges with scissors, taking fresh foliage to pair with my silk flowers, washing the monument, watering the grass, and tending to the young banksia I convinced the council to plant in the nature strip behind the chair.

I don't feel strange anymore, or worried about judgement. I know the people who matter understand.

Every time I go to the cemetery, I write—or read my writing aloud to Coop. When I do, I feel a little closer to him.

It's strange, because I know he's everywhere, and I don't feel a stronger connection there. But I do feel calm.

There are birds everywhere...and I imagine Coop in the spirit world saying, *"My mum's here again!"* to all his new neighbours.
I also imagine him rolling his eyes, saying:
"Mum, what the fuck are you doing here again? Why are you washing my monument?"

But I know there's pride in there too—knowing how deeply he is loved and remembered.

***

This is a world I never imagined. Not for me, and not for anyone who has walked the path of grief.
I had no idea this world existed.

I've made connections at the cemetery—sometimes just a glance across a headstone, sometimes a small exchange of words. Always with a shared knowing: that the pain is real, that the people we love were here, and that they *still* matter.

Cooper...

*Sometimes, sitting there on your chair, pen in hand, I feel the air shift.
A bird lands close by, or a breeze moves through the trees, and I wonder
if that's you—reminding me that love doesn't end here.
It just changes shape.*

Chapter 7
Between Worlds

I'm getting close to going into surgery, and I'm wondering how to explain to the nursing staff that I will probably wake up sobbing.

It's one of those "crazy" people moments. As a bereaved mum about to go under anaesthetic, you wonder if the drugs will allow you to see the person you love.
If your heart stops, even for a few beats, will you get to spend some time with them?
If you have to be resuscitated, could they leave it a little longer—just enough for you to have more time together?

So now you know why I said "crazy."

I don't want to die. I know what death does to the people left behind, and I would never do that to my family—not again. But these are real thoughts. I know I'm not alone in them. Most grieving mums feel the same, even though society would have everyone believe otherwise.

We keep these thoughts to ourselves because we know how much they would hurt the people we love.

I don't want to die.
I want to be here—to watch Ashton grow into the incredible young man he's becoming. He already is, but there are still so many milestones ahead.

What I *do* want is to see Cooper again.

So, when I wake up from the anaesthetic, I know I'll be crying. Crying because I woke up when I thought I might die. Crying because I didn't see Coop. Crying because, as I open my eyes, I have to remind myself again that Coop died.

And crying because the pain I feel—no surgery, no medication—can fix or relieve it.

I just hope I can cry in silence. That the nurses don't try to comfort or console me. It's not a pep talk I need. It's space—to be alone with my grief as I wake and readjust to the reality of my life.

But maybe, just maybe, I'll have the moment I long for.
No words.
No explanations.
Just holding Coop as tight as I can.
He'll feel my love wrapping around him.

Waking up.......... (from the surgery)

That moment I wanted never came.
There was no happy reunion, no hug, no everlasting, loving moment.

I went under the anaesthetic crying.

The anaesthetist had written a children's book, and we'd spoken about it during pre-op. As I was wheeled into theatre we continued talking, and a nurse asked about our books.

When I explained that mine was about loving someone in your

family you've never met, but who you love with all your heart, she asked if it was a personal story.

I started to cry as I said, "I wrote it to honour my son, who died last year—he was 25."

The kind anaesthetist held my arm.
That was the last thing I remember.

When I woke up, I felt so heavy in my sadness. The weight of the anaesthetic mixed with the weight of grief. I felt totally overwhelmed.

It took me a long time to open my eyes.
The last thing I wanted was to come back to reality.

In the days after surgery, I thought about that moment—the space between life and sleep, the tears before and after.

Maybe I didn't see Coop because he is already here.
In every heartbeat. In every breath I take to stay.

Chapter 8
The Ones Who Stay

When you're in a hospital bed, you're generally broken. The medical staff are there to fix something.
When I was in hospital, the staff had no idea I was broken on the inside as well.

It's funny how comfortable people are with the *physical* broken. The emotional broken is far too daunting for most.

I felt like I was living a lie, as they focused on my physical health. I wanted to tell every person that Cooper had died—that life was unbearable without him—and yet I also wanted to tell no one.
I wanted to keep the broken pieces just for me.

What would I say if I did share?
"I am a bereaved mum, broken and unable to be fixed?"
Bereaved mum: what an interesting term. I wonder who came up with it.
Two simple words, one of which once carried so much hope. I remember being pregnant and the power of becoming a *mum*—the joy, the pride, the responsibility. And that was just during pregnancy. When a happy, healthy baby was born, the elevation was indescribable. It felt like the greatest achievement in the world.

But then you add the word *bereaved*, and the pain and heartache are tenfold.
The despair outweighs every other feeling.

And it never leaves.

Mums who are four, ten, sixteen, thirty-nine years into their grief—it doesn't matter—each can be jolted straight back to that moment when the world as they knew it ended. They can still burst into tears without warning, just as they did in the early days. Their bodies still remember the despair of losing their child—losing part of themself.

I remember, years ago, interviewing a family who was enrolling at the school where I worked. It was important in those meetings to build rapport quickly—these families were entrusting us to care for, nurture, and educate their young children.
The interviews I conducted were for children from six months through to five years old.

In one meeting, a mother was very honest with me. Her newborn baby had recently died, and her son, almost three, was struggling to understand.
Of course, I offered my condolences. It's what we do automatically as a society. I told her how sorry I was for her loss and tried to show compassion in the only way I knew how.

Then I suggested something simple: that she could write a letter from the baby to her son—something we could add to his journal, with photos or comments she felt comfortable sharing. I remember her surprise. Her words are still etched in my mind:
"You would let me do that?"

I had no idea then how significant that small gesture was. Allowing her baby to have a presence in her son's life—and not judging it or finding it strange—meant the world to her. I still remember the change in her face, the way her heart seemed to open.

Never did I imagine I would one day reflect on that conversation with such deep, personal understanding. I'm grateful I was able to offer her that moment.

She later told me she'd visited other schools that refused to acknowledge her baby, saying they wouldn't talk about her loss—that it was fine if she wanted to do that at home, but not there.

Now I understand, from the inside, how much these *grief thieves* steal. Their fear shapes their silence.

I often hear people talk about *secondary losses*. The first loss is your child. The second is everything else: family, friends, colleagues, relationships—sometimes marriages. You lose who you were, your income, your plans, your future. The list is endless.

The loss of family, friends, and colleagues is such a shock. Over and over, I hear stories of what these people have failed to do—the hurtful words, the absence, the avoidance.

But I've decided not to focus on these people in my writing. By writing about them, I'd give them more space and significance than they deserve.

We, as bereaved mums, already know they exist. We know the damage they cause—the way we turn their words over in our minds, trying to understand how people could be that way.

I sometimes wonder if they ever reflect on their actions.

Maybe they tell themselves, *"I checked in for a while, but it got too hard."*
Or maybe they convince themselves we were at fault.

The truth is, when your child dies, you have no room for anything else. Even replying to a message takes all the energy you have.

The people we should focus on are the ones who keep sending messages even when we don't respond—the ones with no expectations, who just show love and care.

What I've learned is that often, those people weren't the significant ones before. Some were, but some were acquaintances, distant friends, or friends of friends. Some were entirely new.

So, I will focus on them—on the love, the kindness, the quiet care of those who stayed.

I see it as a privilege to know exactly who my friends are—who I can count on. I have spent a significant amount of time in my life caring for others—now my love and attention are for a smaller circle.

The ones I can message at any time, and they are simply *there*.
No words needed.
Just love.
Or who I fail to message back, and they still show up.

What a gift it is to have these people in my life.

~

In grief, it's not the number of people around you that matters, but the few who understand your silence.
The ones who don't try to fix you—they just sit beside you, in the space where words can't reach.

Chapter 9
When the World Feels Too Loud

Grief doesn't move in straight lines. It circles, it falters, it pulls you backwards just when you think you're finally finding a way forward. And in those moments, avoidance, isolation, and withdrawal become the easiest choices—not because you don't care, but because facing people often feels harder than facing the grief itself.

Thank heavens for groceries being delivered, for Amazon, Kmart, even the library, where I can borrow audiobooks from the comfort of my couch. Because public places are hard now—people are hard. The noise, the small talk, the questions, the pretending…it's all too much when you're holding grief in your chest like a weight no one else can see.

The biggest challenge in walking into any place is the question we've all been conditioned to ask and answer:
"How are you?"

It's the reason I avoid shops.
I don't want to think about how I am.
I am horrible. I'm just existing.

What I've come to realise is that no one actually listens to your response. It's just a polite greeting with no real meaning. What I quickly learned is that you're expected to reply instantly with, "Good, how are you?" and the person answers, "Good."
And that's it.

No one actually asks how you really are.

I've also realised it's not that people don't care—it's that they don't know how to. The question, "How are you?" has become a habit, not a true invitation. And for grieving mums like me, it's one of the hardest questions to answer.

If I tell the truth—that I'm shattered, that every day feels like surviving another storm—it makes people uncomfortable. But if I say, "I'm fine," I'm betraying my reality. So instead, I mirror the question back, and nobody notices that I never really answer.

I wish people would think before they ask. The philosophy should be simple: unless you're willing to sit and truly listen to the response, find a new way to greet people. Maybe say instead, "It's good to see you," or "Welcome."

Leaving the house is hard work.

For the first few months, the three of us stayed together. At the time, I didn't realise how blessed we were to have that. Everything was so bleak. So quiet. We each navigated grief in our own way, but the simple presence of each other brought comfort.

After a few months, Ash returned to school. He was meant to start Year 12 the week after Cooper died. He took all of Term 1 off, and when it was time to go back, I was so incredibly proud of him.

Deane and I couldn't even leave the house—and there was Ash, getting up every day and walking back into the world. He had just turned 18, he had got his licence five weeks after Cooper died. He should have been carefree, living his best life at 18—not carrying the weight of his brother's death on his shoulders.

The fact that he finished Year 12, did what he needed to do, and completed his studies is extraordinary and I am incredibly proud of him.

A few months after Ash returned to school, Deane went back to work part-time, gradually increasing his hours. I can't express how much difference it made having his workplace be so supportive.

When the thought of work—and how insignificant it suddenly feels—consumes you, returning can feel impossible. But Deane's work was part of who he was. It was woven into his core being, and it was also entwined with Cooper's.

They both worked for the same company. Both had personalities that filled a room—loved by many, always making people laugh and feel included. The company was grieving too—for Deane, their friend and colleague, and for Cooper, who had started as a trainee three years earlier and had been promoted to Business Development Manager and relocated to Brisbane just three months before he died.

Cooper's character was charismatic. It didn't matter your role or background—he had time for you.

One of the proudest moments of my life was at his Celebration of Life, when a contractor approached me and said Cooper never cared about the colour of his skin or his culture; he simply saw him as a person.
That's all we ever wanted for our boys—to be good humans.
To be kind.
To be compassionate.

The company recognised the pain of our family and the pain of their staff. In a small workplace, relationships go beyond the office. Cooper had touched the lives of his colleagues and their families too.

He was such an impressive young man—full of potential. I'm so proud of him.

I hold the highest regard for that company, for the way they supported us and their team. I've since learned that kind of compassion is rare.

Deane gradually increased his hours as he was ready. No pressure. No rush. Just an acknowledgment that he was not the same man, and that his team would stand by him as long as he needed.

I remember Deane coming home one day, saying a colleague had told him,
"Your wings were clipped, but they're starting to grow back. It'll take time, but you'll soar again."

That acknowledgment was powerful. It gave him hope—a quiet reminder that healing could exist, even here.

Over time, his wings *have* grown. I don't know how he does it—facing people every day, listening to their problems, when his own pain runs so deep.
I suppose it's that old idea—that he's the man, and he must keep going.

I'm thankful that he does.
Because I can't.

I don't have the capacity to go back out into the world and listen to people's trivial problems. My cognitive function isn't the same. The grief fog is thick and consuming.

Unlike Deane, I didn't have a safe or supportive workplace to return to. That meant my career ended the day Cooper died.

For a while, I tried visiting—seeing colleagues, attending meetings—but it quickly became clear that it was no longer my path. The thought of returning to that space was more damaging than healing.

Nine months after Cooper died, I resigned. I'd been in that company for seventeen years.

My ending was silent.
No goodbyes. No farewells. No letters of thanks.

It was easy to slip away unseen and unheard.
I think it made it easier for others, too.
Saying goodbye would have meant facing the grief, and that's far too hard for many people. So, seventeen years of time, investment, and commitment just ended.

I grieved it for a while. Like Deane, my job had defined me. To lose it brought sadness. But any time I spent being sad about *that* took time away from my sadness for Cooper.

In the early days, I'd wake in a sweat—anxiety flooding in as I tried to comprehend both Coop's death and the end of my career. It was too much.

For my mental health, I had to let go—quickly.

Now I see that ending work was a blessing. I probably would have gone back and let it consume me again, always worrying about everyone else. What I needed was time—time to grieve, to focus on being Ashton's mum, Deane's wife, and to learn how to live as a bereaved mum.

And somehow, in that space, something new was born.
I began to write.
I became an author.
I started my business—*Little Brown Bird*.
I began honouring the 25 years I had with Cooper.

Surprisingly, here I am—about to publish *Do You Look at the Sky?*, reviewing two more children's books, and writing this memoir.

I know now that I will never let a job define me again—except for the roles that matters most: being a mum and a wife. When I look back, I feel a deep sadness for the moments I missed with my family, the times I put work first, the way I was always available to my job when I should have been more present with the people I love. But the truth is, we only realise these things in retrospect—when it's too late to change the past, but not too late to change the way we move forward. Regrets don't help, but they cling to you anyway.

I am committed to helping others see the importance of living first and working second.

It's a saying I'd heard for years—but back then, I thought I had time. Time to make up for missed moments. Time to enjoy their adulthood.

Now I understand why that saying is repeated so often.
Because for some of us, there is no later.

I used to think survival meant returning to who I was before. Now I know it means learning to live as who I am now—broken, changed, but still here.
Still loving. Still writing. Still his mum.

CHAPTER 10
The Day Compassion Went Missing

All bereaved mums have a moment in time they look back on and think: *How did I not lose my composure at that moment?*

When each of us recalls it, others are horrified by the story—but at the time, we're too stunned, too shattered, too exhausted to react. We let that steam train run us over.

Mine was with the funeral manager.

We had just received the news that Cooper was coming home—or rather, that his body was. Even now, I still can't fathom how we survived his death and everything that followed. Coop was travelling from Brisbane back to Berwick, Victoria. The coroner had finally released him, and we could begin to confirm the plans for his Celebration of Life.

It was early morning. Ash and I were driving with Cooper's clothes to the funeral home. Deane couldn't come—the reality and devastation were too much to bear.

On the short ten-minute drive, my phone rang. It was the manager, asking where we were and saying we were late.

Anyone who knows me knows I'm *never* late. I'm the person who arrives early and sits in the car for half an hour, just to avoid being late. I apologised and explained that, according to my notes, we were actually fifteen minutes early. He insisted I was late and demanded an arrival time. I said we were only a few minutes away and that there must be a mix-up with the schedule. I apologised again and hurried to get there.

When we arrived, I was frustrated, thinking maybe I had made the mistake—that somehow I'd let Cooper down.

The manager quickly ushered Ash and I, into a small room and immediately started asking questions about the webinar link for the Celebration of Life. We were using an off-site venue, expecting anywhere between 450 and 650 people.

I explained that the venue had extensive experience and that he should contact them directly. He continued to push, asking technical questions I couldn't answer. Again, I told him to contact the venue.

He began complaining that what he'd set up wasn't "normal procedure", and that he was under pressure from his superiors.

I was stunned. He had been the one to agree to the plan.

I repeated that he needed to speak to my friend coordinating everything or the venue.

He didn't stop.
Finally, I said, "You need to stop. You're upsetting me, and you're not listening."

At that moment, Ash stepped in. My 17-year-old son—who had just lost his brother—looked this sixty-something man in the eye and said, "My mum doesn't have the information you need. She's told you who to contact. You need to follow up."

Basically, my child had to protect me from an adult in authority.

The manager walked out, and a gruff woman entered to record the items we'd brought—Cooper's clothes and the personal things we wanted placed with him. She was cold and dismissive.

I was already shaken, thinking I'd need all my energy just to hand over Coop's clothes and personal items. Then she made an offhand comment about the manager being upset, as if *we* had done something wrong.

As she went through the inventory, I noticed a chest pocket in Cooper's jacket. I asked if she could move the small personal items from the hip pocket to the chest—I wanted them close to his heart.

She sighed. Loudly.

Then she crossed out what she'd written and said, "You want them in *this* one now, right?"
Her tone cut through me.

Ash and I left and drove across the road. I burst into tears.

I had thought, of all people, funeral staff would be kind and compassionate. I realised they were the ones who would *have* Cooper—who would dress him, prepare him, make sure everything was right. It took everything in me, but I called the manager to apologise—for what, I'm not sure. And unbelievably, he continued to complain about his issue.

Still, I ate humble pie. I did what I had to do to make sure everything was perfect for Coop.

Looking back, I can't believe it happened. The lack of compassion. The self-protection. The absence of basic humanity.

I think he made a mistake and was covering himself—but in doing so, every shred of empathy disappeared.

And the saddest part is, almost every bereaved mother I know has a story like this.
Someone in a position of power who should have cared—who made it worse instead.
When I hear these stories, the shock never lessens. The added trauma for mothers already living the unimaginable—it's almost too much to comprehend.

I'm sure that manager has never once thought about the distress he caused. In a role that demands emotional intelligence, how can someone have none?

In the end, self-preservation seems to trump compassion for so many.

But amid all that pain, I have to stop and acknowledge what I saw that day—the strength of my son.

Even in his grief, Ash took on the role of protector. Standing up to a grown man with calmness and clarity. Firm but polite.

It was the second time in a fortnight I'd seen his quiet courage. The first was surviving the unthinkable—losing his brother. The second was reminding a man how to be human.

I've learned that grief doesn't just break your heart—it exposes the world around you.
You see who listens, who turns away, and sometimes, who teaches you what kindness truly looks like.

CHAPTER 11
Grief And The Glass of Wine

Wine became a way of coping.

It's amazing how many mums talk about their relationship with alcohol through grief. It's become a bit of a laugh in our circle—"It's the only way you can get through," someone says, and we all nod. We know it's probably not healthy, but we also know it's real. Sometimes, it truly feels like the only way we can survive another night.

I have to be honest. For almost twenty months, wine was my go-to. It became an easy way out—a small slice of respite. I've always loved a winery visit, a nice glass at dinner, an exclusive bottle shared at a restaurant. But through grief, it became something else: comforting, familiar, easy.

~

In the beginning, I didn't drink at all—which was unusual for me. I needed to feel everything. But over time that changed. I went back to enjoying a drink, then enjoying more, then hoping it might help to numb the pain.

Some nights I'd open a second bottle, knowing it wasn't right but feeling unable to stop. I'd pour myself one more glass, then head to bed. I told myself I didn't need to change because I enjoyed the taste, the brief softening of the edges—and if it helped me fall asleep for a short time, that was a bonus. But deep down, I knew I needed to cut back.

Drinking often made things worse—the pain, the anger, the tears. Words I didn't mean would spill out, hurting the people I loved most. Anything just to escape for a while.

I didn't wake up hungover, not really—just sluggish. But that's grief too. My body adapted to the fog, whether it came from wine or from sadness.

And I need to be honest here—it would be easier to skip this chapter, to keep this part hidden. It's confronting, it's vulnerable, and it might sound like I'm an alcoholic. But this is reality for many bereaved mothers and fathers—and sometimes for siblings too.

It doesn't make us bad people.
It just makes us human.

I recently had a month with no wine—thirty alcohol-free days.
I had to stop, and I knew it. Before my surgery, I promised myself I'd do everything I could to come out the other side healthy—for Ash.

I didn't think I could do it. Habits grow fast, and breaking them feels impossible.
But I did it.

I can't take all the credit—the situation helped. But it gave me space to see that maybe I could live without it.

Now the challenge is staying that way. I don't punish myself for turning to wine—grief already punishes me enough every day. What I do know is that we have to be gentle with ourselves, to remember that this is something no parent should ever have to navigate. Escape looks different for every grieving parent, but at its core, we're all trying to outrun the same thing: the relentless, unbroken ache of missing our child.

Chapter 12
Post-Traumatic Stress

After those first months, I realised the world around me wasn't the only thing that had changed—my body had too. The noise, the panic, the sleepless nights, they weren't just grief. Something deeper was happening.

I didn't know it then, but what I was feeling had a name.

I used to think post-traumatic stress was for war veterans.
Not for me.
Not for the loss of a child.

But now I know—trauma doesn't need a battlefield. It only needs a moment that changes everything.

For me, it's the phone calls. The ones that replay every night, circling through my head like a loop that won't stop.

The first call—*Cooper died.*
The next—*the paramedics,* their voices gentle but final: *"We're sorry, there's nothing more we can do."*
Then the police.
Then the coroner's office.
Each call another piece of the same nightmare.

And even now, all these months later, I can't answer the phone.
It makes sense now—the panic, the tightness in my chest, the way my heart races before I even see who's calling.

Because what if it's *another call?*
What if it's bad news again?

So, I let every call go to voicemail. It's safer that way—I can listen later, read a text message, request an email, take my time, prepare myself.
Emails feel measured. Predictable.
Phone calls are chaos waiting to happen.

PTS.
Three letters I never thought would sit under my name.
But they do now.
I think they'll be there forever—not as a diagnosis I want, but as a reminder of what my body remembers, even when I try to forget.

In the middle of the night, I lie in bed waiting for the worst—a home invasion, a phone call, a knock at the door—my heart racing the whole time. My body is stuck in fight-or-flight mode. It's a state I have become far too familiar with.
Then there are the panic attacks. The triggers are everywhere.
They come at any time, in any place, and even when you expect them, they still blindside you.

Like the time I walked into the doctor's waiting room and saw someone I used to work with, terrified they might try to make conversation. Or at physio, seeing one of Cooper's teachers and wondering if they knew he had died, or if they would ask how he was doing. It happens when an unknown number flashes on my phone and I freeze, waiting to see what message follows.
My body has become so accustomed to panic that it treats it like a constant companion.
It is exhausting.

The flashbacks still come, the calls still echo, and sleep still feels like a risk. But somewhere in the middle of all that noise, I began to crave quiet—a stillness that might let my body rest, even if my mind couldn't. The strain on my heart was becoming too much, living in this constant state of panic was becoming unbearable.

I didn't know what peace would look like, but I knew I needed to find it—even a small piece of it.

Post-traumatic stress leaves you navigating a world that no longer feels familiar. And while I was trying to make sense of that new landscape, I noticed something else—how uncomfortable people are with the truth. Especially the truth that someone has died and how impossible it is to cope with the reality.
But what struck me most was people's avoidance of the words themselves, as if speaking them might somehow make the loss more real. And yet, avoiding the word doesn't protect us. It only leaves us more alone, feeding the very symptoms of PTSD we're already fighting.

Chapter 13
Why We Need to Say "Die"

We live in a world afraid of death—not just of losing, but of naming the loss itself.

When someone dies, the air shifts. Conversations stumble. People reach for words that sound softer, safer. *"Passed away." "Gone to a better place."*
But when we avoid the word *die*, we also avoid the reality of what has happened—and in doing so, we leave the grieving alone in a silence that feels too heavy to carry.

Death is confronting. It changes everything. Yet saying *die* is not cruel—it's real. And in that honesty, there's dignity, clarity, and love. Because to truly support someone in grief, we have to stop pretending death can be softened.
It can't.
But naming it allows us to begin the hard, human work of living with it.

After Cooper died, I noticed how few people could say the word. They'd tilt their heads, searching for something gentler, their sentences trailing into silence.

Some would whisper, *"after you lost him…"* or *"since he passed…"*—as if by softening the language, they could soften my pain. But I didn't need it softened. I needed it seen.

When someone avoids the word *die*, it feels like they're stepping away from the truth that already lives inside me. I carry that truth every moment.
Saying it out loud doesn't make it worse—it acknowledges what's real, and that acknowledgment is a small act of love.

So the question I have is...
Why are we so afraid to use the word *die*?
Why does it scare people?
When I wrote *Do You Look at the Sky?*, a dear friend and early childhood colleague gently asked if I really wanted to include that word—*die*.

I had used the word openly and without hesitation. Their question made me pause. It prompted deep reflection on how we use language around death, especially with children. I appreciated the question and the opportunity to consider why I had chosen to include it.

After much thought, I decided: yes, I'm keeping it in. It felt right. Children deserve honesty. Euphemisms like *passed away, gone to heaven, went to sleep, crossed over,* or even *put down* (for our pets) aren't clear. They're confusing. Children don't sugarcoat their questions—so why should we sugarcoat our answers?

Children are naturally honest. Their world is direct, filled with curiosity and clear-eyed observations. Being truthful about death helps them build a healthier relationship with grief. It gives them permission to ask questions and understand—often better than we do as adults.

I remember when Cooper was little, he used to ask the hardest questions. About where people go. About why people cry. About whether animals feel pain. Even then, he wanted the truth—not a story.
Maybe that's why I feel so strongly about this now.

Society, on the other hand, tends to soften the language. We say things like *"they're in a better place,"* thinking it comforts the bereaved. But does it really? What's real is this: *they have died.* That's what happened, and acknowledging that truth is often the first step toward healing.

So yes—I kept the word in the story. I didn't run from the reality. I leaned into it. Because that honesty helps children process death, and it helps adults too. It gives everyone a shared language grounded in truth.

This reflection returned when I wrote another story—one about plants, animals, and people. When I read it aloud to Deane and Ashton, they were surprised by how often I used the word *die.*

"Children will be terrified," they said.
But children fear what we teach them to fear.
If we treat grief like something to hide from, they will too. If we flinch at the word *die,* so will they.
We model avoidance instead of resilience—just as many of us were taught.

We could learn so much from cultures that allow grief to be visible—where people speak of the dead, cry openly, visit graves, and share memories without shame.

Because the truth is this: when someone dies, they are not coming back. That's the reality. And the only word that truly explains that finality is *die.*

So say it. Use clear, honest language. Practice being comfortable with the word *die.* When we do, we help children understand death in a healthier, more grounded way.

And maybe, just maybe—we help ourselves too.
The word *die* doesn't take away love—it honours it by naming what

truly happened.

So often, people want to help but don't know how.
They soften their words, wrap pain in phrases meant to protect— *"passed away," "gone to heaven," "no longer with us."*

I understand the intent, but those words float above the truth. When Cooper died, he didn't *pass* anywhere quietly. He **died.**

And until we can say that word out loud, we will keep running from the very thing that breaks and reshapes us all.

Saying *die* doesn't take away love—it honours it. It reminds us that love and death are bound together; one cannot exist without the other. The word *die* holds the weight of truth, but also the tenderness of memory. It invites us to face what hurts most and still choose to keep living.

Because when we stop whispering about death, we begin to speak honestly about love.
And in that honesty—fragile, unguarded, and real—healing quietly begins.

Chapter 14
Supporting Someone in Grief

Once people stop hiding behind softened language, they can finally acknowledge the full weight of the loss. Only then can they begin to understand what we as grieving people truly need—presence, honesty, and support that doesn't disappear.

This is written for those trying to help a family member or friend, and for those living with grief. It's for the people standing on both sides of loss—the ones enduring it and the ones helplessly watching someone they love break under the weight of it. My hope is that by sharing these truths openly, we can understand each other a little better, speak more honestly, and offer support in ways that actually help rather than unintentionally hurt.

If you're the one *in* grief—stuck in this tragic hole, drowning—then pass this chapter onto everyone you know, as early as you can. Because the things people say to you...well, some of them are truly unbelievable. Not out of malice, but out of discomfort, fear, and not knowing any better.

What not to say

We all know the old sayings.

We know them *because* we've been through grief, we've probably all been guilty of saying them.

"They wouldn't want you to be sad."

Wrong!

Yes, Coop *would* want me to be sad. I know him better than anyone. He would have judged another mum if she wasn't still sad that her child died.
He'd have said, *"Mum, what's wrong with them?"*

He'd want me to live—yes—but he'd also want me to be sad.
Not consumed by it, but sad.
Because sadness is love that has nowhere to go.

"They're in a better place."

I don't care that they're in a better place.
I don't care if it's extraordinary and surrounded by love.
I'm not there.
I want him with *me*.
Coop with me—that's the better place.

So when *people say* these things, I nod and say, "Yeah, yeah, I know."
I don't agree—I just do it to make them comfortable.

So how do we do better?

What I want you to say in grief is…nothing.
Just *be there*.
Hold me up by being present.

Or say things like:
"I remember how you lit up when you talked about him."

Even if you didn't know him, that's powerful.
It tells me my love was visible. That maybe he always knew that too.

"Sorry for your loss."

It feels hollow when you hear these words; you'll never be as sorry as I am. But I know—it's the safe option. It bridges the awkward gap. They are comfortable to the person saying them.

I've learnt that sometimes I have to break the ice for people. I have to say his name first so *people* feel safe to respond.

That's how this world of grief works.
I say, *"Coop died."*
They freeze—their shoulders tense, the back of their neck prickles.
Then they exhale.
Finally, *"I'm so sorry."*

Before that, I know they weren't even listening—they were just trying to work out what to say.

―

The brave truth

In this world of grief, we, as grievers, have to be braver and stronger, while we are collapsing, chopped off at the knees, unable to breathe.

All we want is for grief to be acknowledged.

Say:
"I can't imagine what it would be like to be you."

Or:
"I don't know what to say, but my heart is broken for you."
Or even:
"I don't know what to say, but I see you. I want to hold you up."

A moment that stayed

One of the most powerful memories I hold is a dinner with two of our closest friends. They'd known Cooper since he was three. They adored him—the cheeky little boy, the sassy teen, the capable, lovable adult.

We talked about their three children and our two. We laughed about the old days.

It wasn't painful—*pain* is the future.
This was remembering.

We talked as if Coop were still here. We didn't have to name the reality. We all knew it.

But I needed to say his name—over and over—because if grief doesn't change love for us mums, why should it change the love others have for him?

As we laughed, my heart filled. They gave us permission to be parents of *two* children—not one living and one gone, but two children we love completely.

I also want to acknowledge this same gorgeous friend who proofread this memoir for me—and who did so much more than that. She was the one who responded every time I said, "I can't do this," answering every call, every message, no matter how much it broke her, because she knew I was more broken.

She was the one I rang and said, "How do I Google funeral homes? I can't do this. I need you."
And there she was.

Her husband was already in Brisbane with us, and she stepped in—researching everything, meeting everyone, making things happen when I simply couldn't.

She later reminded me of a conversation we'd had early on—one I'd completely forgotten in the fog of grief.

She told me that she'd been terrified to say the wrong thing, afraid of adding to my pain—even though she knew that wasn't really possible. She thought about every word.

So I want to say this clearly: I don't write this to exclude the people who tried to help. The people who love you—who show up and keep showing up—have forgiveness.
That's where you start, with everyone.

It's the repeated hurt, the lack of trying, that cuts deepest—not the ones who surround you with love and speak out, even when they're scared of getting it wrong.

That's what matters most: the courage to say something imperfect and still turn up. Because saying the wrong thing and then running—that's way too easy.

Pass it on

Allow the people who sit beside you to read this chapter—the ones who don't know what to say. The ones who speak words that land harsh and raw, not because they mean to, but because they're fortunate enough to have never stood where you stand. I remember being lucky once too—before I knew how deep words can cut.

I remember saying those same things,
thinking they were kind,
not realising how they'd land.

The truth is, you only learn what to say once you've lived deep grief—and I wouldn't wish that on anyone.

Why this chapter matters

This chapter is about enlightenment. About easing the sting of the words that hurt. About protecting the relationships that grief so easily severs—because once broken, they are rarely rebuilt. It's an attempt to share insight: to offer those speaking the words a few tools to try a little harder, and to offer those receiving them a way to forgive a little more.

Chapter 15
The Stillness That Saved Me

After all the noise of grief—the questions, the awkward conversations, the quiet avoidance—I began to crave stillness. Not silence exactly, but a kind of space where I could breathe without explanation.

For so long, my world had been filled with words: words of comfort, words that missed the mark, words that tried too hard to soften what couldn't be softened.

But stillness asked for nothing. It didn't try to fix or protect or explain. It simply held me.

In that stillness, I started to find tiny fragments of peace—fragile at first, but real. Moments where I could feel my love for Cooper without the weight of everyone else's fear or discomfort. It was here, in the quiet, that I began to realise healing doesn't come from avoiding pain. It comes from sitting gently beside it.

When I was working, I supported many of my team through depression, anxiety, and panic attacks. I never truly understood what they were living with, but I knew that support, love, understanding, and acknowledgment mattered.

I never pretended to know how it felt—I simply tried to make things easier. I was always willing to adjust, to change routines or expectations, to help them manage their roles.

What I didn't understand was how *debilitating* those illnesses were. Now I do.

There's the self-hate—the voice that tells you you're nothing, that you can't do what others can. One small doubt and you're at the front of the picket line, shouting your agreement that you'll fail.

There are the stories you repeat at night: that you let people down, that you're too hard to be around. Hate talk and grief crawl into bed beside you, whispering until morning.

I never knew how hard it was for people just to *show up*. I thought a loving and supportive workplace would be enough—a safe, understanding team. I didn't realise that for someone in pain, simply getting out of bed is an act of courage.

My whole life, I just got up and went. But through devastation, I learned otherwise.

In the early days, I didn't sleep—I still don't. I'd be in the living room at 5:00a.m., working on Cooper's Celebration of Life. Going through running sheets, notes, details—using every skill I'd ever had in event planning to give him the best farewell I could.

After the Celebration was over, I turned my focus to the house. Breakfast cooked, house cleaned, dishwasher unpacked, washing done, fire lit, everything done before Deane and Ash got up.

Then Ash went back to school. I was up early, making his lunch, wanting to be there if he needed me.

When Deane returned to work, I'd wake to have coffee with him, make his lunch. I'd never done that before, but if he had to leave the house and face people, it was the least I could do.

Those rituals became anchors.

~

I learned that if I didn't get straight in the shower, I might not leave the bed at all. So I built a routine: get up, make the bed, open the curtains. It meant I'd already achieved something. One small thing in my life was in order.

But as I placed each of the nine pillows and two throw rugs on the bed and made sure the doona was perfectly straight, I'd tell myself: *Groundhog Day.*
The same day as yesterday, and the day before that, and all the ones before.

And the truth was always waiting:
There was still no Cooper.
He was never coming back.
He was still dead.
Just like yesterday.
And tomorrow.
And forever.

~

For me, routines and rituals meant survival.

I've always had a *To-Do List*. Each night I would look at it and decide what I might achieve the next day. It gives me a focus—something other than grief to hold onto during the sleepless hours.

I'd always have a new challenge, like making a flyscreen. I'd lie awake picturing the steps: measuring, mitring the corners, stretching and clipping the mesh. Over and over, I'd rehearse it in my mind, and for a little while, the images of Cooper's death, the phone call, the panic, would fade.

It was a kind of manual labour for my mind—a small reprieve.

***

For the first fifteen months, I didn't stop.
I was always moving—trying to outrun grief.

Maybe that's why my body broke, why I ended up needing a knee replacement. I lived in steel-capped boots, walking thousands of steps every day, hoping a tired, aching body might finally let me sleep.

Wine helped too. It numbed the edges long enough to drift off. But without fail, I'd wake between midnight and 2:00a.m., and if I was lucky, I'd doze again around 4:30a.m.. Then up again by six or seven.

A vicious cycle.

***

I ticked off plenty on my To-Do List—sanding and staining windows, gardening, building, fixing all the little things that had bothered us for years. The house benefited from my restlessness.

I wanted to spare Deane and Ash from more strain. They were already giving all their energy just to function. They worked. They provided. So I took on everything else.

I couldn't see any point in stopping. Sitting still meant sitting *with grief*—and I was terrified that if I stopped, I'd never move again.

I knew I could never return to the work I'd done before. My mind used to buzz constantly with ideas—always thinking about improvements, efficiency, how to help others. It had been exhausting even then.

Now, grief filled every corner of my brain. There was no room for leadership, no space for caring for others. Even leaving the house felt impossible. Facing the *How are you?*'s felt unbearable.

And then there are the milestones.

The anniversaries that keep coming—not just the first Christmas or birthday, but the first *everything*:
The first time a movie is released that Coop won't see.
The first time you drive down a new road and realise he'll never know it exists.
The first time one of his friends becomes a parent.
The first time you achieve something—like writing a book—and he's not here to celebrate.

It's not just the first year.
It's the *first of everything, forever.*

Somewhere around fifteen months, I wrote my children's book. Maybe it was earlier—time blurs, now divided only by BC and AC: *Before Cooper* and *After Cooper*.

I wrote the story for Ashton and for my nieces' and nephews' children. I couldn't bear the thought that they'd never meet Coop—his laugh, his humour, his light.

He was meant to be the first to have children, the first grandchild for six years. Everyone's world revolved around him.

I wondered: How would Ashton explain his love for a brother his own children would never meet?

That's how *Do You Look at the Sky?* was born.

I wrote it at the cemetery—start to finish—in one sitting. The sky above me was stunning. It was mesmerising. I know Coop was guiding me that day.

At first, I didn't think the story was anything special. During a meditation session, I mentioned I had written it, and someone gave me the contact of a self-published author. One conversation led to another—small, serendipitous steps—until I met with a publisher for a review.

She read the story and told me I had something special. She encouraged me to pursue it. I'd imagined traditional publishing, but eventually I enrolled in the self-publishing course, found an illustrator and designer, and months later registered my business: *Little Brown Bird*.

I built a website, wrote blogs, opened pre-orders, entered the world of Instagram, learned content creation, reels, and video editing.

I started a Blog. I found that this—*writing*—was the only way I could sit still.

Writing at the cemetery, working on *Little Brown Bird*—these moments made me feel close to Coop. When I was in that creative space, he was beside me.

It gave me purpose.
It gave me peace.

Thank heavens for ChatGPT as I learned new digital platforms—and for the friends who guided me patiently.

Ash was my toughest critic, always honest about my content. Brutal sometimes, but always right.

Through *Little Brown Bird*, I learned how to be still.
How to sit with grief without being swallowed by it.
How to create in the quiet.

Now, I can sit for hours writing.

In the stillness, I found him again—not in the way I longed for, but in the way love reshapes itself.
Cooper isn't gone. He's here—in every word I write, in every story I tell, and in the quiet moments when the world finally slows down.

Chapter 16
Where I Still Find You

There were other rituals that became important.
Each day, I would shuffle my Angel cards and take one. I truly believe Cooper chose the card I was meant to receive.

One day, I shuffled and drew the same card three times. I didn't want it—it was the one I'd had the day before. Normally I never questioned what came, but on that day I did. Three times, the same card.
I knew then it wasn't a coincidence.

Next, I would open a book of affirmations on healing and take whatever page appeared as my mantra for the day.

Then I'd look at the collage of photos from Cooper's Celebration of Life and say aloud, *"Why the hell are you not here? You are so beautiful. It is so unfair."*

Finally, I'd go into the kitchen and light his candle, his name glowing in the flame.

These small things gave me connection.

~

I've heard other mothers speak about their rituals too—some spend time in their child's room.

Coop had moved out eighteen months before he died. We were so proud of him for taking on grown-up responsibilities. His home was immaculate, everything matching, systems for everything. It was cleaner than his room ever was at home—though I know Beth had something to do with that.

Beth was the love of his life.
I'll speak more about that later.

Initially, Coop was living just one suburb away, so Monday nights were family dinners, with Beth joining us too. There were regular drop-ins to see our two border collie puppies, and moments of ordinary life that felt so full then—we didn't realise how precious they were.

Just three months before he died, Coop was promoted to Business Development Manager in Brisbane. It was a huge decision. He thought about it for a long time—he knew moving away from family would be hard, and he knew he'd be asking a lot of Beth, to move interstate and begin their lives together.

Although Beth was still living at home in Melbourne, they were rarely apart.

He said to me, *"Mum, what do you think I should do?"*

I wanted to say, *"Don't go, stay in Melbourne."*
But that would have been unfair. It was an incredible opportunity. So instead, I said, *"You need to make the decision. Either way you have my support, and I am proud of you."*

Oh, how I've replayed that moment a million times.
Maybe if I'd said *no*, he would have stayed.
Maybe I would have seen him the day or week before he died, instead of a month earlier at Christmas.
Maybe he wouldn't have died.

I can imagine some readers rolling their eyes. I've been told so many times that nothing would have changed—that we all have a "death date."

It doesn't matter.

As bereaved mothers, we rehash these moments endlessly. You can tell us we're not responsible, but as mothers, we will always feel guilt—that we couldn't change what happened, that we couldn't save our child, that, somehow, we should have done something, anything, differently.

Only mothers who have lived this understand what we put ourselves through.

Rituals are important.

For some, it's sitting in their child's bedroom or touching their belongings.

For me, it's being in nature.

We bought our block of land when Cooper was three. Every weekend we spent on site—cleaning, preparing, gardening, hanging out in the shed. When the house started to be built, we'd drive past on the way to school and again on the way home.

When it was at lock-up, Cooper would climb through an open window to let us in. He'd role-play in the empty rooms that would become our home, collecting nails and screws, climbing dirt mounds, building cubbies, fighting dragons, casting magic spells, creating potions.

His imagination was extraordinary.

My reprieve now is the garden.
It makes sense—we spent so much of our lives in that space together.

Nature has always been part of me. I've developed bush and beach programs for early learning for years, but now I understand it differently.

Connecting with the earth, with Mother Nature, is *essential*.

Being in the garden is where I feel closest to Cooper.
The wind, the sun, the rain, the storms—all remind me of the power and significance of nature.

It's even reflected in *Do You Look at the Sky?*

Cooper and Ashton were both outdoor, adventure boys, part of the Surf Life Saving Club. Coop especially loved climbing trees.

When he was little, we went to Emerald Lake Park for his birthday. The trees there were enormous—nothing like at home.

All he wanted was to climb them. I didn't mind—he knew his limits (or at least, I thought he did).

He scurried up quickly, face glowing with pride. Some older people nearby muttered that it wasn't safe, that I shouldn't allow it. I pretended not to hear them.

Watching his joy as he reached the ground again was unforgettable.

That day we rode Puffing Billy, had cake and presents and a picnic—but the highlight for Coop was the tree.
That memory never left him.

～

As a surf lifesaver, Coop was one with the ocean.
The waves were no deterrent—he met them with ease and strength.

Deane often speaks with pride of Coop's power during his first surf lifesaving challenge, completing his Bronze Medallion effortlessly.

Cooper started swimming lessons at six months old. He was a natural—a duck to water. The swim school adored him. It was no surprise he became school swimming captain and still holds records there.

When Coop was 12, we bought a house at Cape Woolamai on Phillip Island—our weekend escape.

Every day, he'd plead to visit "the pinecone trees." They hung over the cliff face, impossibly high, but he'd climb them anyway—fearless, imagination alive.

Ash, seven years younger, would watch in awe, wanting to be just like his big brother.

～

Nature followed us into later years—jet-ski adventures on the island, private beaches, family camping trips on the Murray River.

Whether it was wakeboarding, jumping off cliffs, or just floating in the icy ocean, Coop was happiest outdoors.

Right now, I'm sitting outside, looking at the blue sky, the clouds drifting, the wind on my face. And I feel him here.

There are endless memories of our family in nature. It's no wonder I feel Coop everywhere when I'm outside—especially in our backyard, among the plants we planted together, the cubbies he built, the magic he imagined.

Being in the garden, at one with nature, is where I feel closest to him.

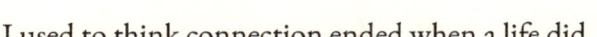

I used to think connection ended when a life did.
But now I see it differently.
Love doesn't vanish—it transforms.
And when the wind moves through the garden, I know he's there, reminding me to keep looking at the sky.

Chapter 17
Spirit on Country

I'm not alone in sensing Cooper in our backyard. Murrindindi, the *Nalegeta* of the Wurundjeri People, feels his spirit too.

As soon as Murrindindi heard about Cooper's death, he sent a message: whatever we needed, he was there for us.

I have been blessed to share a deep, personal connection with Murrindindi over many years. He opened his heart and allowed me to learn about his people and culture. He gave me permission to share these learnings with educators, embedding Indigenous perspectives in teaching and curriculum. Our friendship grew from mutual respect and genuine care.

When his message arrived, I knew the significance of it—an Elder offering support to our family, a non-Indigenous family, but one that had long been an ally and advocate.

~

In the beginning, we weren't sure how to include an Indigenous perspective in Cooper's Celebration of Life. It was something that felt important to all of us, yet we'd never seen it done—not in Indigenous or non-Indigenous ceremonies.

The more I thought about it, the clearer it became that we needed Murrindindi's presence. I asked if he would do a Connection to Country for Cooper.
There was no hesitation. His "yes" came with love and genuine concern for our family's wellbeing.

~

On the day of Cooper's Celebration of Life, Murrindindi wore his possum-skin cloak. The significance of an Elder wearing his cloak—of him standing there with us—was overwhelming.

But even more powerful was knowing it was *him*—a man I deeply respected, admired, and loved. He spoke in the Woiwurrung language—the traditional language of the Wurundjeri people—and sang a song taught to him by his grandmother.
He spoke of Bunjil, the eagle and creator spirit, who would watch over Cooper, protecting him as his ancestors came to meet him.

The moment was extraordinary.
It lives within us still—the comfort of knowing that Indigenous ancestors are protecting my boy's spirit.

After years of learning and teaching Indigenous perspectives, I realised how deeply that respect had become part of who I am.

~

When the service ended, Murrindindi walked ahead of the hearse carrying Cooper, leading the way. Behind him, the bagpipes played—a nod to our Scottish heritage—the perfect harmony of cultures, history, and spirit.

I am so proud to call Murrindindi family. He has continued to support us for almost two years—visiting, calling, and offering healing.

He has come to our home and told us that he sees Cooper's spirit moving through our backyard.
He brought a healing *yidaki* (didgeridoo) and played it as part of a smoking and healing ceremony around our fire, joined by our extended family and Beth, on Cooper's birthday.

He later lent us a *yidaki* to keep in our home—to encourage Cooper's spirit to visit. He has spent time with Ashton, teaching him how to play, showing him care and understanding, knowing the pain of losing a brother.

It takes an extraordinary person to continue to call, to check in, to visit—to keep showing love and genuine concern. I will forever be grateful for our friendship, for all he has done for our family, and for all he has done for Cooper.

It's through these experiences that I know Coop's spirit is strong and present in our backyard. When I see Bunjil soaring overhead, I feel peace—gratitude for such a strong connection to the spirit world.

I'm thankful that years of learning from Indigenous culture have become ingrained in who we are as a family.

It reminds me of the contractor who spoke at Cooper's Celebration of Life—telling me Coop accepted everyone for who they were. I smile, knowing this openness lives in all of us.

Reflecting on this reminds me that faith takes many forms. I didn't grow up religious. The only times I went to church were with friends, when staying over at their homes.

When I began working at a Christian school, my interest grew. I spent time learning with the Chaplain and helped develop an early-years Christian curriculum with colleagues. I became comfortable talking about God and Bible stories.

But when Cooper died, my faith shattered. I thought being a good person meant we were safe and protected.
Suddenly, I questioned everything.
Nothing made sense.

I stepped further and further away from the comfort I had once found in Christianity.

My connection to Indigenous spirituality is what brings me peace now—and I love that Deane has embraced it too. He's always the first to spot Bunjil circling above us, pointing the spirit out in the distance.

Faith comes in many shapes and forms.
It's different for each of us.
I'm blessed—I have my Elder, my guide, walking beside me on this journey.

My previous thought that connection ended with death changed, I realised that it deepens—through wind, song, spirit, and story.

The land itself carries his memory, whispering it back to me each time Bunjil circles overhead.

The Indigenous beliefs about spirit, connection, and the continuity of life offered me a way to breathe again—a way to imagine that Cooper was not gone, only changed. Their wisdom grounded me in something larger than my own grief, something ancient and steady.

But understanding the spiritual world was only one part of survival. The other part was learning how to live in this world—the world without him—and finding ways to soothe a body and mind that had collapsed under trauma.

Chapter 18
The Price of Healing

When everything hurts, you look for anything that might ease the pain.

I remember visiting my GP—an extraordinary woman who has supported our family with a holistic approach to health for many years. She helped us raise healthy boys and became someone they trusted. Of course, being boys, they didn't always agree with her advice, but they respected her completely.

On the night Cooper died, I emailed her and said Ash needed someone to talk to. From that moment, she became more than our doctor—she became a confidant, present in our lives in ways that went far beyond medicine.

Now, when I walk into her office—changed, not the person I once was—she sees me. She acknowledges who I was, who I am now, my broken heart, my love for my boys, and my effort to stay strong for Deane and Ash. She understands that sometimes it's one breath at a time—and that even breathing can be hard.

∼

One day, I told her, "I think I'm having heart issues. It beats so fast, and it's physically painful. I think I'm having a heart attack."

I had never heard anyone speak about the physical pain of grief before losing Coop. I didn't know sadness could feel like this.
I was wrong.

This was the price of love.
Great love equals great pain.

Like many grieving mums, I tried anything that might ease the strain on my heart. I didn't understand how it could keep functioning under so much strain. Apparently, it can—even if it's changed forever.

So, I began exploring alternate healing.

~

I'm blessed to have a longtime friend who, just weeks after Cooper's Celebration of Life, gently brought me back to Pilates. She called the studio ahead of time to explain what I was going through. For the first few sessions, she made sure it was just the two of us. We said almost nothing, and I cried through the movements.

Being given that space—in a familiar place, without pressure—allowed me to reconnect with my body and my grief.

Almost two years later, that same dear friend still gets me out of the house twice a week. Every single time, we meet in the car park and hug. She's seen the rawest sides of me. She's never tried to fix me. She always speaks Cooper's name—with love, with memories—and she lets me be whoever I need to be that day, feel whatever I need to feel. She is such an extraordinary friend.

~

And oh, the millions of messages that came and continue to come. Simple words that reminded me I was still someone, still loved, still standing.

Never underestimate the power of checking in, or of being the one who keeps showing up.

There are many paths to healing.
I've been fortunate that everything listed below has helped me in some way—though much depends on the skill and heart of the person providing the care.

Things That Helped

People often ask what helps when your child dies.
The truth is, nothing truly helps—not in the beginning. But over time, you start to find small things that hold you up for a moment, and those moments matter.

These are some of the things that helped me:

Writing

Putting my feelings into words became my lifeline. Sometimes it was just a single sentence in a notebook. Other times, pages poured out. Writing didn't fix anything, but it gave the pain somewhere to go.

Nature

Being near the ocean—walking, watching the waves, feeling the wind—gave me a sense of peace I couldn't find anywhere else. The rhythm of the tide reminded me to keep breathing.

The Compassionate Friends

Finding others who truly understood changed everything. There's a comfort in sitting with people who don't try to fix you—they just get it. They hold space for your pain without needing to make it smaller.

Stillness

In the quiet—wrapped in a blanket, a cup of tea beside me, breathing slowly—I found moments of calm. Grief is noisy, but stillness reminded me that I could survive one breath at a time.

Bilateral Music

I started listening to bilateral music—the kind that moves gently from one side to the other, left to right, right to left. It's used in trauma therapy, especially with war veterans and people living with PTSD.

The sound shifts between ears, helping the brain process memories that are stuck, the ones that replay over and over. I use a soft headband with flat speakers, so I can listen as I fall asleep.

The science says it helps rewire the brain's response to trauma. For me, it feels like a quiet rhythm that steadies the chaos—almost like my mind is finally being rocked to rest.
It doesn't erase the memories, but it makes them less sharp, less loud.

Sometimes, healing is found in the smallest things—like sound moving gently from one side to the other, reminding my brain that it's safe now.

Support People

Friends and family who kept showing up—even when they didn't know what to say. They didn't try to fix it. They just stayed. That's all anyone in grief really needs.

Time

Not in the way people mean when they say, "time heals."
Time doesn't heal—but it creates space between the waves, space where you can catch your breath. And slowly, those spaces start to fill with small moments of light.

Faith in Love

Not religion—love.
The quiet knowing that love doesn't end when life does. That's what keeps me moving forward.

These are not solutions—they're reminders.
Small things that helped me survive the unbearable and begin, somehow, to live again.

Other things I tried—and were helpful—included:

- Reiki
- Spiritual guidance from Murrindindi
- Sound healing
- Meditation and mindfulness

- Chiropractic care
- NET (Neuro Emotional Technique
- Mediums and psychics
- Massage
- Psychology

What I've learned is that *healing is expensive.*
Many of these therapies aren't covered by health insurance. I've chosen to invest in them—to be a better human for those who have to, or choose to, be around me.

But what about other bereaved mums?
Everyone should have access to the supports that might help them survive.

―

The only therapy I truly struggled with was EMDR—Eye Movement Desensitisation and Reprocessing. It focuses on traumatic memories while tracking eye movement, designed to desensitise the memory and reduce triggers.

I tried it four times in a month. For me, focusing on the trauma made it worse. I left each session exhausted and more depressed.

Deane tried EMDR and found it incredibly helpful. It softened his traumatic memories, allowing him to revisit them without pain.

Everyone is different. There is no right or wrong.

Just like grief—each of us experiences it differently, and what helps one may not help another.

Other things that have helped me:

- Journaling
- Physical activity
- Gardening
- Time at the cemetery

It would have been easy to get a prescription for medication. Depression often equals script. But for me, no pill could fix the pain.

I chose not to go down that path. Partly because I enjoy wine—and, honestly, because I wasn't ready to give it up—but also because I've always leaned toward natural health.

When the boys were little and got sick, we'd go to the chiropractor for realignment or try acupuncture and Chinese herbs. It's how we lived—holistically.

I know many mums who take medication, and I honour that choice. What's right for one person should never be judged by another.

I remember when I used to advocate for chiropractic care—how people would rush to tell me I was putting my children at risk.

What a judgemental society we live in.
Everyone thinks their way is the only way.

How about we simply accept what people need—and trust them to know what's right for their own healing?
Do what is right for *you*.

Read. Ask questions. Make informed choices.
But most importantly—listen to your gut.

Learn from the experts, not the haters of the world.
And above all, do what is right for *you*.

Healing isn't about fixing what's broken.
It's about finding the strength to keep loving, even when your heart hurts.
And sometimes, it's about knowing when to rest—and when to rise again.

CHAPTER 19
The Weight of Paperwork

Nothing prepares you for what many bereaved mums call "Death Administration."

It's the mountain of paperwork and bureaucracy that follows your child's death. The forms, the signatures, the endless questions.

For those of us whose children were young adults, there's no Will, no power of attorney, no pre-arranged wishes.
How many parents have sat down with their 25-year-old and discussed cremation, burial, or finances after death? You might have planned these things for *yourself*—never for *them*.

We had no idea of Cooper's wishes.
We didn't know the state of his finances.
He had just moved interstate.
Everything in his life was in transition—beginnings, not endings.

～

The number of decisions we were suddenly forced to make was staggering.
I'll leave the list aside for now—it's too heavy.
This isn't about logistics.
It's about the *pain* that comes with them.

What I didn't realise at the time—not fully, not until recently—was how constant and cruel the burden of administration is.

The reason I was shielded from much of it is because my sister and brother-in-law stepped in. They went into *battle*—and I use that word deliberately, because every process was harder than it needed to be.

Every step brought another form, another signature, another statutory declaration.

They did everything.
They took the burden.

They were the ones who, in every phone call, had to say the words: "My nephew died."

They had to recite his date of birth and date of death, over and over.

They had to say where he lived, where he died.
They were the first to receive the email addressed to the family of *"The Late Cooper Reid."*

They absorbed the full force so we wouldn't have to.
Then they came to our door—quiet, gentle, hearts breaking—to tell us what needed to be done next, to get another signature, to soften the blow before it reached us.

They stood in the storm so we could breathe. They took the hits so we could survive. There are no words for that kind of love.

We were blessed beyond measure to have them.
Some of what they achieved would have been impossible for others.

Even something as simple as a flight refund became a fight. My brother-in-law had booked our flight to Brisbane. When we arrived at the airport earlier we were told we couldn't transfer to an earlier flight, only pay for a new ticket. There was no compassion, no understanding. We didn't care—we just needed to get to Ash as quickly as possible.

My sister persisted. Out of principle, she made them see reason. Why should grieving parents be penalised?

When she tried to cancel or claim small refunds on Cooper's bills, she'd say, "It doesn't matter how much—it's Cooper's money, and he worked hard for it."

They were determined—to support us, to honour him, to fight the unnecessary battles we couldn't face.

At the time, I knew what they were doing was huge. But I only understood the full weight later, after hearing other mothers' stories.

Recently, for the first time, I had to submit Cooper's death certificate myself. Almost two years later—and still, the pain was unbearable.

Holding that document felt like holding my own vulnerability. How dare an organisation ask for something so personal, so final?

I realised then how much my sister had protected me.

Even now, there's still that slap in the face—the reality of death administration. Sometimes it comes weeks later, sometimes years.

A new Medicare card arrives in the mail and you realise your child—their name, their number—has just been removed. No warning. No explanation. Just gone. Deleted with the click of a button, as if a person could be erased that easily.

When I contacted the Minister about it, a Medicare staff member called me. She explained that Cooper had been removed because he was "no longer current."

No longer current.

Well, he is very current in my life—as is every other child whose mother has to endure this process.

Oh, what an ambivalent world we live in.

The staff member went on to tell me she understood grief. And I wanted to scream down the phone, *"Did your child die?"* But I didn't. I stayed quiet.

Then, months later, another letter arrived—an error, they said. "Sorry, someone pressed the wrong button."

But that single mistake breaks your heart all over again. Because how do you not know? How can you not understand that my child's name isn't just a record in a system—it's my whole world.

～

I hope every mother who walks this road has someone to be their Death Administrator—someone strong enough to absorb the blows and face the bureaucracy for them. Don't try to do it alone. Lean on the people who love you. They want to help—let them.

There were two occasions when organisations refused to let my sister speak on my behalf, even though I had signed the forms, written the emails, completed the stat decs. I told them she could provide all the answers—that I couldn't speak.

But at their insistence, I had to. Both times, I took the call, shaking, hysterical, unable to say much more than my name.

I remember breathing through sobs and finally saying, "My son died. What more do you want me to say?"

There was silence. Then the condolences, the apologies—and magically, a solution. Suddenly, they found a way for my sister to manage it after all.
It wasn't the individual's fault—they were following company protocol.

But there *should* be guidelines for how to handle these situations—frameworks that protect grieving families from being retraumatised by policies that lack compassion.

I will always be grateful to my sister and brother-in-law—for their strength, for their endurance, and for their love.

They fought the systems so we could survive the sorrow.

Because the truth is, the paperwork doesn't just record death—it repeats it.

Every form, every phone call, every signature forces you to relive the moment your child left this world.

And that is the cruellest part of all.

The world keeps moving in straight lines—paperwork, policies, procedures—

but grief doesn't follow rules.
It loops, it circles, it repeats,
until love becomes the only language that still makes sense.

Chapter 20
Through the Fog

"What's my name?"
It's not a trick question.
Where do I live? When was I born?
They become questions that can stump you in an instant—leave you feeling like you're no longer in control of your own life.

The only thing that sits clear at the front of your mind is:
Cooper died.
28 January 2024.
25 years old.
Happy. Healthy. Living his best life.

Those are the things you know.

I'd heard of perimenopause and menopause fog—I'd even laughed about it with friends. But grief fog doesn't pop in for a laugh. It's forever present. It's debilitating.

Someone's name. What you ate yesterday. All a blur.

In the early days, I didn't know where I was half the time. People would talk, and I'd nod, but nothing would land. I could hear the words, but I couldn't make sense of them. My brain was like static—a low hum that drowned out everything except the pain.

Grief fog.
I didn't know it had a name then, but that's what it was. It's not just

forgetting where you put your keys or what day it is. It's walking into a room and forgetting why you're there. It's staring at your phone, trying to remember who you were about to call. It's reading the same line over and over again and not understanding a word.

It's your brain's way of protecting you—cushioning you from a reality too heavy to carry all at once.

In those early months, I lived inside that fog. Time didn't make sense. I'd wake up and not know if it was Tuesday or Sunday, March or June. I'd forget conversations, appointments, even names of people I'd known for years.

And with every slip, the guilt would come: *How can I not remember? What's wrong with me?*
But nothing was wrong with me—or with any of us who grieve this deeply.

The brain just can't process the unthinkable. It slows everything down to survival speed. It's like trying to move through water—every thought heavy, every action taking effort you don't have.

I remember trying to fill in forms—and I'd write the same thing twice or forget what I was meant to sign. I couldn't even string enough words together to explain why.

Sometimes I'd start sentences and not be able to finish them. Words would vanish halfway through.
And yet, I was still functioning—still walking, still breathing, still cooking meals, even if I didn't remember doing it.

It's strange how your body keeps going even when your mind has stopped.

The fog lifted slowly, in its own time.
Not all at once—more like a dimmer switch. Little flickers of light

coming back.
I'd remember things again, make a plan, feel a flicker of lightness—briefly—and then it would roll in again.

That's how it works. Grief fog doesn't have an end date. It just softens with time, but it is always still lingering.

Now, when I meet other bereaved parents and they talk about how forgetful they are, how tired their minds feel, I tell them:
It's not forgetfulness. It's protection.
Your brain is doing what your heart can't yet manage. Be gentle with it.

I started to find ways to live with it.
Lists became my lifeline—on paper, on my phone, wherever I could write them quickly.
Journaling helped too, even if the words were messy and out of order.

Routine mattered—making the bed, feeding the dogs, lighting Cooper's candle—small anchors to keep me from floating away. And when I couldn't think clearly, I learned to stop expecting myself to.

The fog isn't failure. It's love trying to find a way through shock. It still rolls in—unexpected, quiet.
I'll lose track of a day or forget what I was saying mid-sentence. But I don't fight it anymore. I know it's just my heart and my brain taking a moment to catch up with each other.

I used to think grief fog was weakness. Now I see it for what it is—grace. It's the space between devastation and survival. The place that gives us time to breathe before the next wave hits.

And if that's not strength, I don't know what is.

Chapter 21
The Gift of Preparation

One of the things Coop taught us is the importance of being prepared—of having the difficult conversations about death and dying.

It broke my heart when Ash said to me,

"Mum, when you die, Coop was meant to be here doing it with me. Now I'll be alone."

Even now, writing those words, I cry. It still breaks my heart.

That moment changed me.
I realised that love also meant protection—even from the practical pain of loss.

I began documenting everything: every contact, link, password, account. I created a funeral file, with all the decisions made.

Ash can change whatever he chooses when the time comes, but he won't have to *decide* unless he's ready. Every choice is written down—a roadmap for when the world feels impossible to navigate.

We have the family plot at the cemetery and the monument, ensuring we can all be together again one day. It's an option for Ash and his future family, if they wish.

I still can't believe we had these conversations with our 17-year-old son. It felt like life had fast-forwarded—childhood to adulthood to death—all at once.

How could our conversation shift from turn 18, find love, marry, have children, and then...speak about death.
What the hell.

Now, when I speak to people, I tell them:
Cooper's gift to you is the reminder to have the conversation.
Make the plans.
Because if you don't, your family will be forced to make those decisions in the worst moment of their lives.

Since Cooper's death, our entire family has begun planning.
My parents found a spot in the Rose Garden beside my grandparents—miraculously still available after all these years. Friends have started creating their own files, exploring burial and cremation options.
Discussions are happening. Decisions are being made.

I encourage everyone: make death talk *comfortable*.
Allow your family, when the time comes, to focus on *grieving*, not on decision-making. We all know how quickly unmade decisions can divide families.

Think, too, about funding your funeral.
Accessing money quickly can be difficult—especially for your children with young families.
Even if you believe there are funds available, can they actually be accessed right away?

Death is a business.
There's no "pay later" option.
It becomes another cruel burden for families already in shock.

Planning is meant to be for the older generation. No parent should ever have to plan their child's funeral.
We're meant to be paying school fees, buying first cars, helping with weddings or house deposits—not negotiating the cost of a coffin.

If this is you, I am so sorry.
All I can say is: it's one cruel world.

Death doesn't only shatter parents.
It fractures entire generations.
And for a long time, I couldn't see past my own grief to recognise anyone else's.

Chapter 22
The Forgotten Grief

I need to take pause from my grief to talk about grandparent grief. It's something I've only recently had the space to consider.

How could I possibly have thought about someone else's pain when my own was consuming me?

But now, with distance and reflection, I see it.

~

Calling my parents—and Deane's—that day was the most heartbreaking thing I've ever done.
It destroyed their world.
It was a different kind of pain—layered, deep, generational.

I can still remember every word of those conversations.
They're etched into me forever. But I keep them locked away, deep in a filing cabinet in my mind. I know they're there, but I can't bear to take them out.

~

In the beginning, it was hard for me to even be around them. Their sadness was written all over their faces—the heartbreak, the disappointment, the helplessness.

I felt like I had *failed* them.
It was my job to keep my children safe, to keep them alive. I couldn't bear the thought of them looking at me and seeing what I imagined to be my failure reflected in their eyes.

Of course, it wasn't what they felt—but it was what *I* saw.

Now, having spoken to both our mums, I understand their grief differently.

For them, it's the imbalance of nature that's unbearable.
They were meant to go first.
Their grandchildren were meant to remain.
They were meant to be the ones greeting them in death—not the other way around.

We also had the complication of distance. My parents live in regional Victoria, four hours away.
No dropping in.
No spontaneous hugs.
No quick cup of tea and tears.

Every visit required planning, overnight stays—usually with my sister and her family. The three of us—Deane, Ash, and I—were barely holding on. We couldn't have anyone in our space for long; it would have broken us further.

So, although we were close, *being close was hard.*

When our parents were with us, they had to hold it together—for us. They became the steady ones, the protectors, even as they grieved their grandson.

I remember a grandmother at The Compassionate Friends support group saying her daughter didn't want to spend time with her anymore. In that instant, something clicked for me—a lightbulb moment.

I realised, when I looked at my mum and my mother-in-law, I wasn't just seeing their grief for Cooper—
I was seeing their grief for *us.*

They lost their grandchild, yes—but they also lost *their children.* Because they knew our happiness was gone forever.

They saw all the years of love, effort, and stability—28 years of marriage, a home, security, dreams for the future—evaporate in a single moment. All they wanted was to take our pain away. To make us whole again. But no deal, no wish, no prayer could do that.

The reality for them is that their own children—*we*—will never again know the kind of happiness we once had.

Every layer of grief teaches something new—about love, about survival, about how far pain can reach.
But through it all, I keep coming back to one truth:

Love doesn't end. It just changes form.

Chapter 23
Sibling Grief

Sibling grief is its own kind of devastation. The loss of your brother...
How does a heart endure that?
It's a pain that settles so deep that only siblings can truly understand its shape.

Even writing these words feels unbearable. The weight of them presses on my chest, and part of me still can't believe they belong to our story.
So I don't want to linger here for long.

Cooper was an only child for seven years. I'd always believed that if I became pregnant once, I would end up with two children, and knowing he was a twin probably deepened that quiet belief I'd always carried. I had lost his twin early in the pregnancy.
My Pa was an only child. He used to whisper words of guidance, "It's tough being an only child," but it never really bothered me. Cooper was perfect. So why did we need to go back?
And then, of course, we did. Thankfully.

Along came Ash—seven years later.

The boys always complained they should have been closer in age. They used to say they'd be better friends if they'd grown up with less of an age gap. But the truth is, it doesn't matter how far apart your age is—that bond finds its rhythm when the time is right.

My sister and I fought like anything when we were younger. Even as adults there were extended times we didn't speak. But through this grief, I've realised how much she means to me—how she held me up, supported me, stood there at every turn.

When I read all the quotes about sisters—the ones about being each other's anchor—I understand them now. It brings me such comfort to know that I have that closeness.
But it also breaks me to think that Ash has lost that.

He was just getting to the age where he and Coop had become best mates. They'd reached that sweet spot—laughing about us, teasing Deane and me, calling each other to say, *"You won't believe what they've done now."*

They had their own lens—the shared jokes, the history that only siblings understand. Those memories that come from being in the same world, in the same moment and seeing it all together.

You think that will last forever—that you'll share it for the rest of your life.
And then it's gone.

It breaks me to think that Ash had that—and lost it so early.

The weekend Cooper died, he was the big brother taking care of his little brother—showing him the ropes, sneaking him his first sip of Scotch at 17, giggling like they always did, away from us, caught up in their own world.

They were so close.

Sibling grief feels like it takes a back seat. As parents, we're so consumed by our own pain that we forget—they've lost their *forever*, too.
Ours was a forever of raising them.
Theirs was a forever of *growing up and growing old* together.

They planned to be best men at each other's weddings. They talked about being the cool uncles to each other's kids. They'd joke about the nursing homes they'd choose for Deane and me—saying we'd better be nice to them because *they'd be the ones making the decisions.*

That kind of future—those shared dreams—they don't disappear, but they change shape. Cooper will still be part of Ash's life, just differently now. He'll be missing from every milestone, every chapter, every laugh—but always watching.
Always near.

CHAPTER 24
Key Dates

I don't know if it's the dates themselves, or the expectations that come with them, that I fear most.
Each one feels heavy—another reminder of what's gone, another day I have to survive.

Mother's Day

The first big day for me was Mother's Day.

How was I supposed to be present for Ashton, when half of my heart was buried with Cooper? Deane and Ash were both terrified of what the day might bring. Everyone around us gave me space—the usual family expectations were gone.

But when people asked, *"What do you want to do?"* I didn't know. How could I think beyond the heartbreak?

I woke up full of dread but tried to hold it together for Ash. He needed his mum too. He looked like a small boy again, terrified that he might break me—feeling somehow responsible for making me feel special.

I told him no presents—I didn't want anything. But he still gave me a beautiful card. Such beautiful words.

Now that Cooper's gone, any words he wrote on cards have become precious. A few days earlier, I'd found one he'd written, tucked away in a place I never expected.
It was like he was saying, *"Mum, you're still my mum. I still love you."*
I was home alone when I found it and broke down completely.

Ash's card that Mother's Day meant more than any gift could. Each word written with love and tenderness.

I rang my mum, and Deane called his.
I ended up in tears—too much pressure to talk, to be grateful, when I just wanted to hide. But I also knew Mum was alone, so far away, and probably crying at her end too.

Father's Day

Then came Father's Day.

I didn't know how to support Deane. He seemed stronger than me, but I could see it was taking everything he had, just to get through.

We saw his dad that week. My parents were away travelling. It was quiet. We all just moved through it carefully, as if the air might shatter.

Birthdays

Then came my birthday—three days before Cooper's.

I used to laugh that once Cooper was born, my birthday stopped existing. I became the add-on to his celebration. Now, I don't care if I never celebrate it again. Each year feels like another reminder that I'm getting older, and he never will.

On his birthday, messages of love arrived, and friends sent flowers. I spent time at the cemetery—alone.
That's how we cope now. We visit separately. We don't need each other's grief in those moments; the time feels more sacred alone.

I was grateful for the messages from friends. It's the day Cooper blessed this world, and I will always celebrate that.

I cooked for two days straight—a feast for our families. Murrindindi and Beth joined us. We felt Cooper's presence in the backyard, connected through spirit.

Deane went to work, but he couldn't stay. His team had organised a "KFC Day for Coop." Cooper loved KFC. It was all too real.
Ash went to work—it was the distraction he needed.

Christmas

Then came Christmas.

The year before, Cooper had come down from Brisbane—a grown man visiting home. It hadn't been our best Christmas, but it was our last as a complete family.

Now with no Cooper, it felt hollow.
Why were we buying presents?

After throwing away so many of Cooper's things, we couldn't bear to fill our house with more. You realise how much of life is clutter—how we collect "things," only to leave them behind.

Friends sent messages of love. Some were hesitant, and that was okay. No one knows what to say.
But the most important thing they can include is Cooper's name.

That's what Christmas is now—survival.

Deane and Ash insisted I put up the tree. Cooper loved Christmas. He loved my OCD tree, and he loved decorating his own once he moved out. I didn't want to do it, but as with so much in grief, we do things we don't want to.

I avoided the shops—the happy people, the music, the forced joy. If I couldn't buy it online, it wasn't important. I stayed home.

New Year's Eve

Then came New Year's Eve—Cooper and Beth's anniversary. Another broken moment. Nothing to count down, nothing to look forward to.

And then the new year—another cycle of dates to face again.

Mother's Day.
Birthdays.

Christmas.
All over again.

And still to come: 18th and 21st birthdays, engagements, weddings, milestones that should have been his too. Deane turned 50 five months after Cooper died. Ashton turned 18 five weeks later. My dad and then my mum both turned 70.

Cooper loved a good speech—he always spoke off the cuff, always heartfelt. The absence of his voice at those milestones made the silence heavier.

No one knew what to say. Every celebration ended in tears, with a gap that could never be filled.

Survival—that's what these key dates are now. You never really know what you need, or what you want others to say. You just hold on for the ride, and hope that somehow, next time, the waves will be a little gentler.

After each milestone, I felt emptied—like I'd held my breath just long enough to survive the day. The exhaustion that followed wasn't just physical, it lived in my bones, my heart, my mind.

The 28th January

Then came the lead-up to the one-year mark—and even that phrase feels wrong. The word anniversary suggests celebration, something marked with joy or achievement. It makes a milestone of something that should never have happened. Anniversary is not the word I choose for Cooper's death day. It is simply the 28th of January. The day our world shattered.

How do you possibly survive one year of losing your child?

Ash went to work—always the safest distraction for him. Our boys had learned from us that work was the constant, that it mattered, that throwing yourself into it wholeheartedly was what we did.

I spent the day in the garden, wandering around in a daze—not crying, just heavy. I remember feeling utterly lost, unable to comprehend how this had become my reality.

Later, the three of us ended up at lunch together, at Cooper's favourite place—the same venue where we had held his wake. There was a quietness between us, a shared effort just to survive the day.

Simple hearts continued to appear on my phone—small messages from people letting us know they were thinking of us, knowing how broken we were, sending love in the only way they could.

What will this day look like in the years ahead? I honestly don't know, but the second anniversary—I hate that word—is quickly approaching. The boys will be busy with work—Ash with a new job—and life will continue to move around us, even when we can't. There will always be an awkward silence as this date approaches. I know they will worry that I'll break. And they're probably right. Year after year, I will break again and again.

What I do know is that we will never acknowledge this date the way others do. There will be no rituals, no marking of a milestone. For us, the silence is what matters. The quiet is the only space that feels respectful, the only thing that feels bearable. But every family is different.

I do know this: Like the sunrise and the sunset, this day will keep coming. And for us, survival is all we can hope for.

CHAPTER 25
The Group No One Chooses

It was about three months after Cooper died when my friend said to me, "I will be by your side forever and I will do whatever I can to support you, but I will never truly understand what you're going through."

She went on, "Do you remember when we first had our boys? The only people who really got us—who knew the sleepless nights, the endless crying, the exhaustion—were those going through it at the same time. It was our mothers' group."

Then she said, "You need to find that group of people."

It was such wise, heartfelt advice.

~

After searching for some time, I found *The Compassionate Friends*. The first group I attended was filled with mothers who were older—many had grandchildren. I left in tears, knowing I couldn't go back.

I felt robbed of that future. Cooper had always wanted to be a dad, and Beth had hoped she was pregnant—she'd even been so unwell we thought maybe she was—but she wasn't.

I couldn't sit in that circle and listen to stories about grandchildren, knowing that I would never have that piece of Cooper living on in the world.

～

Then one day, I caught up with someone from work. In the past I would've called her a close colleague, but now I realise she was just a colleague.

She said, "You look really good."

And I thought, *What a crappy thing to say.*
Just because I'd brushed my hair and put on makeup that day—you tell me I look good? I wanted to scream, *I feel like shit!* But instead, I smiled and said thank you.

How easy it is to fake it. How much better it makes others feel when I look like I've got it together.
What a joke.

I got in the car and drove straight to *The Compassionate Friends* drop-in centre in Canterbury—an hour away.

～

When I walked in, a kind and compassionate lady greeted me. She had lost her daughter. We sat together for two hours and just talked.

For the first time, I felt like my pain was visible. My brokenness on the inside could finally be seen—not hidden behind the polite façade I used to make others comfortable.

～

At my first official support group meeting, I was welcomed with open arms by the mums who knew this kind of grief.

I could barely speak—I couldn't form the words to describe my loss—but they knew. They recognised the pain.

As we went around the circle, I noticed that some of their pain had softened slightly with time. People kept saying, *"You're so early in your grief."*

And I thought, *It doesn't matter how fresh it is, it's always going to feel like this.*

Now I know: It doesn't go away.
It just changes form.
The pain becomes familiar.
And with time, you learn how to carry it.

～

At the start of each meeting, the creed is read aloud—a simple reminder that this room is safe, that our feelings are valid, that nothing goes beyond those walls.

At the end, we stand in a circle with a candle in the centre. We put our arms around each other and say our children's names—with pride, with love, with grace, and with heartbreak.

It's a moment of unity and confusion all at once—that quiet awareness that none of us ever imagined being here, yet somehow, here we are.

～

I've continued going every month.
Deane, Ashton, and my sister sometimes worry that the meetings bring the pain to the surface, but the pain is *always* at the surface.
The meetings don't make it worse.
They give it a place to go.

This is a group none of us ever wanted to join.
But it's a group I'm so grateful for.

These women are my new friends—my lifeline.
They hold space for me.
They acknowledge my pain.
They don't try to fix it or pat my knee to make it better.
When I say Cooper's name, they hang off every word, because they know what it means to speak love out loud.

In this circle, I am Vicki—Cooper and Ashton's mum.
That's who I am first and foremost.

Connection with these mums has been my anchor.
When I said I wanted to write a children's book, they cheered me on.
They understood the significance of it—not just for me, but for their own children, their own legacies.

When I read the story to them, the room filled with support. They said, *"You have to do this. Cooper would be proud."*
There were no questions about why or how or what it would cost—just encouragement, love, and belief.

I have the utmost respect for these women.
They get out of bed each month, show up, and share their deepest, most intimate truths without hesitation.
They show up for themselves and for each other.

And every month, I show up too.

Because I know the healing that happens in that circle—the love that fills that room.

I wish every mother walking this path could find a space like this—safe, understanding, sacred.

But I also want to say, from the bottom of my heart:
I'm so sorry you're here, part of a group we never chose to belong to.

Chapter 26
The Auntie Heart

How do we manage our different roles through grief?

I've always loved my role as an Auntie.
My sister has two children, and my sister-in-law has two. I adore my nieces and nephews.

We've always been close. The kids grew up spending time together—especially at sleepovers at Grandma's and Nann's house. They adored Cooper. Being the eldest cousin, he was idolised. He always had time for each of them—especially the girls. Maybe it was because he never had sisters of his own.

I'm also Godmother to my sister's children, a role I've always treasured.

Through grief, I've been constantly torn. I've always wanted to be someone they could trust and confide in—someone they could turn to if anything was happening in their lives. But after losing Coop, I was overwhelmed with my own grief.

How could I support them through their loss of him, when I had no capacity to manage my own?

I don't recall much of our early interactions—it's all fog. I know we hugged a lot. I know I couldn't find words. I couldn't be the one to comfort them. I was barely managing to breathe and keep living myself.

Now, as time has passed, I see the distance that has grown between us, and it deeply saddens me—especially when there is already such a huge gap in my life.

But it's not something I can force or fix. I just need to keep showing up—to be here when they're ready.

Sometimes I think about how impossible it would have been if there were younger children in our immediate family.

I admire the mothers I know—and those I don't—who have had to navigate grief while raising little ones.

Teenagers retreat. They need space and time to process. They need quiet.
But young children—they don't stop. They don't pause to give you a second to breathe. There is no quiet.

If that's you, please know this: You are extraordinary.

Find moments of quiet where you can.
Try guided meditation together. Even very young children can manage this.
Lay outside in the sun and watch the clouds.
Let them tell you what they see.

Use sensory materials—clay, paint, sand—to let them express what can't be said in words.
Spend time in nature, at the beach, in the garden, under trees.

If you have young children and you have lost a child, you are amazing.
Be proud of yourself.
You are doing the hardest thing there is—loving through the silence, surviving through the noise, and keeping your heart open enough to keep giving love, even when it's broken.

Love doesn't disappear—it simply shifts its shape.
I see it in my nieces and nephews, in the kindness of friends, in the small ways life keeps offering reminders that connection remains.

And perhaps that's what legacy truly is—love, finding new ways to stay alive.

Chapter 27
A Love Lost Too Soon

I take a breath before I write and reread this chapter. Even now, my chest tightens and my heart swells. There are parts of grief so tender you hold them gently, they are painful yet comforting at the same time.

I could fill pages and pages—but my point here is simple:
to talk about *unexpected connections*, and how friendship and love can grow through grief.

―

Beth was the love of Cooper's life.

The week before he died, Beth had called in to see me while Cooper was working in Brisbane.
I said to him on the phone later,
"Beth is a special girl, mate. She loves you wholeheartedly. Is she the one?"
He gave me a very *Cooper* response—changed the subject, avoiding any talk about feelings.

A few days later, I said it again:
"She's special, Coop. She really loves you."
He laughed and said,
"Mum, you already told me that."

Coop and Beth met during COVID, so their relationship began in a bubble—focused entirely on each other, sheltered from the world. They were opposites in many ways, and that was good for him. They challenged each other.

Beth had already committed to moving to Brisbane.
Cooper and Ashton had been building her furniture, following sketched layouts and assembling pieces via FaceTime, with Beth directing every detail.

The boys spent the weekend cleaning—preparing for the next chapter of their lives. It was just over a week before Beth was meant to drive north and relocate.

Then the unthinkable happened.

When I made that call to Beth, my hands shook, my vision blurred. I didn't know how to say the words—they just fell out of my mouth. I don't even remember if it was fast or slow. It wasn't compassion. It was shock. Pure heartbreak spilling out before I could form anything gentle.

She already knew something was wrong. Coop was always on the phone—constant messages, Snapchat, check-ins. The silence was deafening.
We all imagine the worst sometimes, but you never imagine *this*.

I can't really explain how Beth and I navigated our grief in those first days.

All I knew was that Coop loved her—and she needed to be part of as many decisions as possible.

When we didn't know whether to choose burial or cremation, we turned to Beth.
She and Coop had talked about it before, after both her grandfathers died.

I gave Beth every opportunity to be involved, wherever she wanted to be.

When she sent me her reflection for the Celebration of Life, I thought, *There's no way she'll get through reading this.*
It was the most loving, raw, tender tribute—and yet she did it.
I held my breath watching her stand there, fragile and fierce. She poured her heart out in front of hundreds, almost collapsing from an illness we didn't yet know she had, and she was admitted to hospital later that day.

She made Coop proud.
It was a testament to their love, and to the life they were meant to have.

At Cooper's Celebration of Life, Deane told everyone, with such tenderness, that Beth would always have a place in our family—and he meant it with all his heart.

After that, Beth and I continued to message each other—holding one another up, trying to survive the silence where Coop's voice had once been.

On Valentine's Day, she sent me a message that I'll never forget:

"You were the first woman he loved. You taught him how to love."

For Mother's Day that year, Beth brought me flowers and said they were from Coop. (I'm crying again just writing that.) The foliage from those flowers is still alive—not growing, just surviving.
Like a reflection of us both.

Beth shared photos and videos with me—glimpses of their life together I'd never seen. Some were vulnerable and intimate; others were filled with laughter and mischief—Coop driving her crazy with his brotherly pranks. Thank heavens she had grown up with a brother—she knew exactly how to handle him.

She's joined us for a few family dinners following his death, where we would reminisce about better times.
The dogs always excited to see her. Her bond with Ash is still like the brother-in-law I know he would have been.

We've walked and talked, shared lunches, cocktails, and dinners—cried through movies when the triggers came. We can say the "crazy," inappropriate things to each other that we can't say to anyone else.

Beth has come to every family milestone, just as she would have if Coop were here. Each time, it feels like she brings a piece of him with her.

We've gone to the island together, retraced old memories. She still tells me new stories—small things about their everyday life.

Once, I burst into tears because I couldn't remember Cooper's favourite ice cream. I knew what he'd loved as a child, but not as an adult. Beth answered instantly—with the flavour, and a story to go with it. Such generosity.

~

I recently read *Death Do Us Part* by Lauren Zonfrillo who wrote about her stepdaughter and herself becoming *grief partners* after losing her husband.

That's what Beth and I have become.

A friendship has grown from our shared love of Cooper.

I told her I needed to stop introducing her as my son's partner—and start saying *daughter-in-law*.
She should have been.
For now, we've settled on calling each other *family*.

~

I'm not sure we would have been this close if Coop were alive. Maybe we would have had the typical mother-in-law/daughter-in-law dynamic—a little polite distance. We both smile, wondering what Coop would think of our friendship now.

If he were here, he'd probably roll his eyes—we'd team up against him. But I think he'd be happy.
Happy that we have each other.

~

This friendship is a blessing.

I've spoken to other mothers whose children's partners drifted away after death—or where hurt turned into division. Beth and I worked hard to make sure that never happened. There was never competition over our love for Coop. We chose *love* over everything else.

Even now, as I write this, Beth and I are messaging back and forth. She's offered to take me to the cemetery while I can't drive after my surgery.

~

My heart warms and my tears well when I think about her.

I know that, in time, Beth will meet someone new.
It's what I want for her.
It's what Coop would want for her.
I have no doubt.

She shares her stories with me—little updates about dating, life, new hopes. I love that she feels comfortable enough to be open.

Sometimes she'll say things like,
"This guy is really career-driven—like Cooper."
How beautiful, that she still honours him that way.

~

For Beth, that day changed everything.

She lost her future—the move, the job, the house, the dreams of marriage, children, and a lifetime with Cooper.

She lost her second family too—the dinners, the holidays, the laughter. Though we've kept much of it alive, it's never the same.

She probably would have been a Reid.

~

When I hear of bitterness between mothers and their children's partners after death, I think: *Try a little harder.*
You've already lost so much.
Don't lose more.

Because if you can find love—or even forgiveness—you will gain far more than grief can take.

~

Though the stories may come less often now, that time in our lives is carved deep into both our hearts.
We'll always be connected—not by marriage, not by blood, but by love.

Thank you, Coop, for finding this beautiful woman.
She will always be the love of your life.
And I know you'll always be her guardian angel—watching over her, her family and over all of us.

~

Love doesn't end.
It just finds new ways to stay—in friendships, in stories, in the people our children loved.

Through Beth, I see glimpses of the life Coop was meant to have—and somehow, that keeps him near.

CHAPTER 28
Men's Grief

This is an additional chapter I decided to add.

I spoke with the builder working at our house. He was removing a mirror, and I remarked that he could take the bad luck with him—I'd had enough of it.

That small comment opened the door to something much deeper. As we talked, I told him about Cooper.

He paused, then quietly said that his stepson—the boy he'd helped raise for fourteen years—had died.
And that was it. The building work stopped for a while. We both stood there, two strangers suddenly connected by the same unthinkable loss.

He told me his marriage had broken down after his stepson's death. Grief had driven a wedge between them, one too deep to repair.
The pain on his face said everything. It had been five years for him, yet the ache was still raw.

Our conversation deepened my understanding of how differently men experience grief. I already knew this from watching Deane, but now I saw it through a new lens.

For so many men, it's not that they don't feel the pain—it's that they don't feel allowed to show it. They go back to work quickly, because that's what's expected.

There's pressure to be strong, to provide, to keep moving.

They see their partner's heartbreak and feel helpless to fix it. It's an impossible burden—wanting to protect, but not knowing how.

I could see it in his eyes: the exhaustion of holding it all in. He told me he no longer had his wife to talk to, and now had a new partner. I couldn't help but think how complicated that must be—how you navigate loving someone new while still grieving the child from a previous chapter of your life.

He said he thinks about his stepson every single day.
Just as I think about Cooper.

Through our conversation, it felt like I gave him permission—permission to speak, to be seen, to be heard.
For a little while, he wasn't just a tradesman; he was a heartbroken father, missing his boy.

He'd lost not just his stepson, but also his marriage, his home, his sense of normality—all the things that help you survive grief. And I couldn't help but wonder: At what point does grief become so heavy that the longing to be with your child outweighs the will to keep going?

Later, when I told Deane about the conversation, he shut it down. I got the exact response one man gives another—quick, deflective, uncomfortable. It reminded me just how differently men and women process their pain.

As I sat in the garden afterwards, the sun warm on my face, the dogs at my feet, I thought about it all. I felt something—a familiar nudge, that quiet whisper from Cooper saying, *"Mum, you can do this."*

Over the previous two days I had meet three people who had lost their children, how do you explain that? The tradesman the third.

Maybe it's no coincidence.
Maybe it's another reminder that my ability to listen, to guide a conversation gently, to acknowledge someone's pain—maybe that's what I'm meant to do.
Maybe this is how I can help.

Grief wears many faces—some silent, some loud, all real.

Men hurt deeply too; they just need space to be seen, without needing to be strong.

Chapter 29
Grief, Marriage, and the Space Between Us

One thing Deane, Ash, and I have in common through this grief is that we all chose to see a psychologist. I was determined each of us should find someone we could connect with—someone who could help us navigate this unimaginable pain.

Each of us had different levels of success. I'm the only one who has continued monthly therapy (more often in the beginning). It's been over twenty months now.

But I'm proud of my boys.
So many men don't speak to anyone.
They see therapy as weakness instead of what it really is—a tool to survive, to grow, to protect relationships.

~

Deane came home from one of his sessions and told me the statistics on marriages that fail after a child dies. As had happened to the builder. We both agreed—we didn't want that to be us. But there were times it was so hard to understand each other's grief.

My grief is loud.
Emotional.
Visible.

I cry. I break.
He can't fix it—and that breaks him.

His grief is organised.
Tucked away.
Processed in his mind and heart in different compartments so he can function.
That's how he protects his memories and his love.

We had to learn to respect and understand each other's grief styles.

That sounds lovely in theory, but in reality, it looked like this:

It's Saturday night. We're watching a movie.
A trigger hits me—I'm sobbing.
Deane says, "I need to change the channel. This is too hard."
And I'm thinking, *That's not the point!*

Do we scream?
Do we walk away?
Do we hold each other?

There are no instructions for this.

The thing that kept us going was reminding each other:
We're not alone. We're just different.
And different is okay.

It didn't always feel good to hear this reflection, but it snapped us back to reality—we were still together.

Sometimes I cry all day—at different triggers, or just once—and when I tell Deane, I see him shut down.
Not because he doesn't care, but because he cares *too much*.
He wants to fix me.
He loves me so deeply that watching me hurt makes him angry at the world.

He believes his job is to protect me—to protect the mother of his children.
When he can't take away my pain, his love comes out as frustration.

So I hide my emotions.
Not because I'm dishonest, but because I don't want to hurt him.
Sometimes it feels like grief makes me live a half-truth.

If he asks, I'll be honest.
If he doesn't ask... Why make him carry it?

Instead, I go to others—my friends, my mum, my sister, my psychologist, other grieving mums.
It feels like living in a parallel universe.

Deane and I have always been open, passionate, heart-on-our-sleeves people. We've never been afraid of "battles"—the good kind—debating, pushing, fighting for what we believe.

But now I find myself crying quietly, looking away so he can't see.
Same room.
Heavy heart.
And he's unaware.

Not his fault.

I'm just trying to protect him.

~

I've realised I'm not alone in this. So many grieving mums do the same.

In a strange way, maybe it helps. It forces me to hold it together a little longer, to dig deeper for strength, to reach for strategies I know are there but don't always use.

Sadness is my default.
Grief is my language.
But maybe learning to *hold it* sometimes is part of the journey too.

~

Despite everything, I know we bring out the best in each other.
I know we are strong.
I know Cooper wants us to love each other forever—and we will.

Both of our parents are incredible role models—long, happy marriages, strong families. We've always said how lucky we are to have that example. It set the standard for us…
and sometimes it hurts knowing that bar was also set for Cooper.

~

Grief and marriage.
Grief and relationships.
Grief and love.

And yes—grief and sex.
(That's a whole other chapter I'll never get to... But it's real. And it's hard.)

Everything is hard.
But we keep choosing each other.

Because as painful as it is to do grief together...
doing it *together* is still better than doing grief alone.

Grief tests everything—love, faith, friendships, even your sense of self.
But when it strips everything back, what's left is truth.

Chapter 30
Sleep, Surrender, and Small Awakenings

Sleep.
It's totally underrated.

I've always been someone who tossed and turned through the night—my overactive brain thinking about work, family, life, to-do lists. My mind was busy, never fully at rest, but it felt productive. I'd often wake with new ideas, goals, or ways to support people better.

But for almost twenty-one months...I haven't truly slept.

~

I can go to bed late, completely exhausted—after hours in the garden or working on projects—and yes, I might collapse into sleep faster than usual. But it never lasts.

Without fail, I wake at 3:00a.m. Nine times out of ten.

I'm sure Cooper died at 3:00a.m.
I woke at that exact time the day he died. I sent the boys a message: "Everything OK?"

I don't know why—maybe it's that middle-of-the-night connection mothers have—but something in me knew.

Months later, I noticed Cooper's clock. I'd hung it in his old playroom, which had become the boys' media room as they got older. It wasn't about the time—it was just there.

Then one day, I realised: It had stopped at 3o'clock.

Maybe I could dig deeper to confirm his time of death, but honestly, it doesn't matter.
In my heart, I know.

So when I wake at 3:00a.m., sometimes I think—it's him nudging me.

He was like me. He had insomnia too. He could stay awake all night. The only difference was, as a teenager and young man, he could sleep half the day away. I can't.

Sometimes I'm awake for hours. If I'm lucky, I might get six hours of sleep in total—but it's broken.

You don't realise how that slowly erodes every part of your body and mind. It affects everything.

The only reason I truly understand the importance of sleep now is because of my last night in hospital, in rehab following my knee replacement. After all the signs (which you'll read about in a future chapter), I slept—almost eight hours. Straight.

Yes, I turned. I felt my knee pain. I was aware of it.
But I didn't get up.
I didn't look at the clock.
I just... slept.

And when I woke, I was ready to cry—not from sadness, but because I felt *different*.

The pain in my knee wasn't as bad.
But more importantly, the pain in my heart wasn't as heavy.

~

I got into the shower expecting grief tears. But none came. Instead, I felt relief.

One insightful nurse had told me,
"You need to let him go. Your sadness might be holding him back."
At the beginning, I believed that. I tried to stop being sad so he could move on—because I knew he wouldn't want me devastated.

But my sadness changed over time.
It wasn't just devastation—it was *closeness*.
It was *love*.

How do you choose how to grieve, when grief is how you love?

~

But that morning... I could breathe a little deeper.
My heart felt a little softer.
It didn't feel so hateful.

And when I say "hateful," I mean that quiet, heavy anger that simmers underneath:
Why did this happen to my son?
Why us?
Why our family?

Letting go of that, even just a little, made more room for love.

Maybe this won't make sense to anyone else. Maybe it won't even make sense when I read it back later.
But right now, in this moment, I feel proud. Proud to be Cooper's mum.
And a little bit proud of myself, too.

Because for nine days—three in hospital, five in rehab—I've had to interact with people over and over again. I've had to let my light shine while they cared for me. I wanted them to see gratitude, not grief.

Rehab for my knee gave me time to focus on my body, but it also gave my *mind* a break. The rhythm of people coming and going, meeting new faces, being in a different environment—it helped my whole wellbeing.
Maybe my surgeon had insight I didn't have.
Maybe I needed this space.
A place to escape—even briefly—from the depths of grief.

I know there are grief retreats, but I don't think I could sit for days focused only on loss. Here, I had to focus on *healing*.

So as I head home—
I feel tired.
I feel grateful.
And I feel...insightful.

Maybe, just maybe, sleep is part of how I find my way back to living.

Chapter 31
What I Was, and What I've Become

What I was, and what I've become, are worlds apart.

I look at the executive suits lined up in my wardrobe, and the almost one hundred pairs of shoes stored neatly beneath them, and I wonder—what do I do with them now?

I loved dressing up for work.
Now, I live in the garden.
My wardrobe has completely changed.

There's my garden tracksuit.
My house tracksuit.
My Pilates tracksuit.
And my *going somewhere* tracksuit (like to the psychologist or Reiki).

My sister tells me to leave the suits there—that I'll need them when I'm doing my book launch or public speaking events. She's so sweet. But I don't actually think they'll fit anymore.

When Cooper died, I lost so much weight, almost overnight. How can you eat when you feel sick all the time? Then, eventually, food became my comfort.

Taking care of people made me feel useful. So, I cooked—three meals a day, baked snacks for Ash (who is *always* hungry), and baked for my support group meetings. It was my way of showing love—through my hours and hours of cooking and baking.

Then came the coffees, the morning teas, the friends who dropped by with cakes and treats. The kilos just kept coming. There was nothing I could do to stop it.

Walking became difficult with my knee, so the suits now just sit there, with all their colours and fancy fabrics—stunning, but purposeless.

It was recently pointed out to me that the suits no longer fitting might be a metaphor for something deeper—the emotional misfit of trying to step back into a life that no longer feels like mine. I'm not the same person anymore. Will I ever fit into the world I once did, or into the suits I once wore?

~

Our social life disappeared too.
The work functions, the networking, the professional dinners—all gone.

The executive in me was gone.
What was left?

A hollow shell.
Still a wife. Still a mum.
But I felt like I wasn't doing a great job at either.

Now, I was a housekeeper.
A cleaner.
A gardener.
A renovator.

A chef.

That's what I was *good at* now.

And then, new roles emerged:
Skywatcher.
Dreamer.
Memory keeper.

~

For so many years, I had passion. Purpose.
I was an advocate, a leader. I had a clear vision for my career and for the difference I wanted to make.
I always said I'd *never* stop working—I loved it too much.
It seems funny now, thinking about that version of me, so certain about working forever.
What was I thinking?

Now, all I can focus on is survival.
And maybe—just maybe—being an author.

~

I never thought I'd say those words out loud.
It felt like a pipedream. A passion project.
Certainly not something that would actually happen.

I said *author* out loud for the first time in hospital.
Someone asked what I did, and it felt like a safe answer after six days of uninterrupted writing.

Successful? Published? They didn't ask for details.

Just, "What do you do?"

And I said,
"I'm an author."

What I *do* is remember.
I love.
I miss Coop.
I dream of a different time—
a better time—
when he was still in this world.

Maybe this is who I am now—
not the executive, not the planner, not the one with all the answers—
but the one who writes, who remembers, who feels.

Maybe that's enough.

Chapter 32
The Comfort of Fur and Faithful Eyes

When I think back over the past twenty-one months, I can't overstate how important our fur babies have been—our two border collies and our Persian cat.

Cooper loved them so much—sometimes I think he loved his dogs even more than he loved us. He would call home just to see the puppies.

We'd had two border collies before these two, and Cooper was devastated when they died. He was at home with each of them when the vet came, and as heartbreaking as it was, there was something peaceful about their final moments before death being in the comfort of their own home.

The ashes of our two collies, Bandit and Dusty, rest with Cooper in his casket. When I later spoke with a psychic, she told me, "Your dogs are with Cooper."
I didn't need convincing—I already knew he'd be happy to have them by his side.

Not long after Cooper died, I remember looking at our dogs, Marlo and Chloe, and asking them, "Where's Cooper?"
Then I stopped myself. They weren't searching for him—they still saw him.

Sometimes they'll do something so peculiar in the backyard that I can't help but wonder if Cooper's out there playing with them—tossing the ball, rolling in the grass, doing all the silly things he used to do that broke every bit of training, just because he loved them so much.

Animals sense grief. They always have.
Since losing Cooper, they've become even more affectionate and attuned.

Even our cat—who has never particularly liked me and has always adored Deane and Ashton—started sitting on my knee. She'd never done that before. It felt like she could sense the heaviness in my heart and wanted to ease it.

Over time, my dogs have almost forgotten how to be dogs. Their connection to me is so close now, it's as though we breathe together. Since I rarely leave the house, they're always beside me—inside if I'm inside, outside if I'm outside.

Even now, as I write this, Chloe is lying near me, her little face resting on the bed, paw hanging over the edge, watching me as if to say, *"I'm here if you need me."*

My parents recently got a new puppy. Their old dog died not long after Cooper, which broke their hearts.
Though yes, it was "a dog," that grief reignited the pain of losing Cooper. The only comfort was imagining their dog reunited with him.

Around that same time, they both saw a soft glow near Cooper's tribute in their house—something they couldn't explain. I've heard that when a pet or family member is dying, our loved ones often come to greet them and guide them home.

I can't help but wonder if that's why Mum and Dad saw Cooper's light just days before their dog died.

Watching them fall in love with their new puppy has been healing. It's something to care for, to love, to hold, and to look forward to.

We can never underestimate the power of animals in our lives. They teach us how to love without words, how to comfort without fixing, and how to simply be there.

I think about therapy dogs working with children and the comfort they bring. I feel so blessed to have had these fur babies through my grief—loyal companions who've carried me through some of the darkest days with nothing more than presence and love.

Sometimes the most healing souls don't speak our language—they just listen, stay close, and remind us that love never truly leaves.

Chapter 33
The Power of Love in Action

I want to share some of the positive, meaningful acts of support we experienced after losing Cooper—because most people *want* to help, but don't know how.

These simple gestures carried us.
They still do.

I once heard a phrase: "Grief groceries."
It might sound unusual, but it's the perfect description.

One day, a friend arrived with a car boot full of groceries—fresh food, pantry staples, comfort treats, things we never would have thought to buy. It was a full weekly shop.

No fanfare.
No questions.
Just love.

It was an extraordinary gift—a true act of kindness. Inside were essentials for visitors, comfort items for us, and most importantly, a silent message:
"We can't fix this...but we are here."

Since the 28th of January 2024, I've received a message on the 28th of almost every month from a dear friend.

Sometimes it's words of love.
Sometimes a quote.
Sometimes just a heart emoji.

Simple. Consistent. Powerful.

It reminds me that my pain is seen, that Cooper matters, and that I'm not alone.

Cooper's work colleagues came together and gathered every photo they could find of him, putting them on a USB for us.

So many selfies. So many memories.

They were proud of him and loved him—not just as a co-worker, but as family. There were photos we had never seen before.

That gift was priceless.
No words can fully express our gratitude.

Sometimes the doorbell would ring and no one would be there—just a crockpot of food, a salad, a home-cooked meal on the doorstep.

No pressure to talk.

No expectation.
Just: "We want to take care of you."

Those meals lowered our shoulders. They removed one more decision from an already overwhelmed mind. Each dish was filled with love and hope.

People we barely knew—friends of friends, members of community groups—sent prepared meals, checked dietary needs, and made sure we were supported.

The reach of Cooper's life was wide.
So many people were touched by him.
So many wanted to honour him.

Yes, the flowers were beautiful, and they came with heartfelt messages. Our home looked like a florist. We felt deeply loved.
But flowers fade.
And they changed how I see cut flowers now—they became tied to grief.
That's why, at Cooper's Celebration of Life, we asked people to donate to Woolamai Beach Surf Life Saving Club—the place Cooper loved—instead of sending flowers.
It was meaningful.
And it felt like him.

What I've learned is this:
Love isn't about grand gestures.

It's not about money.
It's not about being front and centre.
It's not even about the funeral.

Love is:

- Saying their name, even months later.
- Remembering important dates.
- Sending a message when everyone else has moved on.
- Showing up in quiet, gentle ways.
- Letting grief be witnessed, not fixed.

It's these small, thoughtful acts that mean the most.

They don't take the pain away...
But they remind us we don't have to carry it alone.

These small gestures—meals, messages, photos, donations—became lifelines. They taught me that love isn't what you say. It's what you *do*, quietly, again and again.

Chapter 34
Messages from Beyond

Not long after Cooper died, I was reminded of something I'd never really thought much about—mediums and psychics.

One of my closest friend's daughters went to see a medium, and Cooper came through.

The psychic told her Cooper was insistent, almost pushing and shoving his way forward to get a message to me. He wanted her to tell *his mum* and *his girlfriend* that he was okay.

My friend hesitated to tell me at first, unsure how I'd react, but something I said opened that door. The next day, I was on the phone to her daughter, listening to every word.

I shared the experience with Beth and my family, who were all blown away. Even so soon after he'd passed, Cooper was coming through so strongly—something the medium said was rare, a sign of his strength of character.

～

I know this might not sit comfortably with everyone, but I can tell you this: I live in a family of non-believers who now believe.

They've each had experiences that changed their understanding. Both my mum and mother-in-law have had Cooper's name flash on their phones as if he were calling—even though his number was disconnected shortly after he died.

My parents, who were never spiritual, both saw him independently—a radiant light near his tribute table, on the same night, each afraid to mention it to the other until later, fearful of sounding foolish.

Months later, my sister heard a well-known medium, Cael O'Donnell, on the radio and convinced me to go with her to a live event. I was hesitant—still raw, still sceptical—but I agreed.

Cael was remarkable. He had this energy, this presence. As he moved through the audience, he began describing a young man who had passed suddenly—a brother, a spirit connected deeply to the ocean.

He said the spirit had followed him all day, desperate to get through. Then he started describing details: a young man who was here and then gone, just like that; who'd previously had an injury in his left eye; he was living somewhere different to where he grew up; he loved a particular pair of shoes—shoes so distinctive that his best mate had taken them after he died.

He spoke of the funeral, a reflection that was unique and moving, something tied to love and culture.

My heart pounded. Every word felt like Cooper.

I looked at my sister. I wanted to raise my hand, but I was terrified.

Then Cael looked directly at us, standing less than a metre away, on the step just below our seats, he placed his finger to his lips, and whispered, "Shhh, shhh, Mum."

He continued, "You had a date when you were supposed to make a change to your work—you still haven't done it. You must make that change."

He said this spirit was with his mate—maybe Cooper's friend who had died two years earlier—that they were together, like having a drink at the pub, and that he was at peace.

I left there knowing it was him. The details were too personal, too specific.

I tried contacting Cael later to see if spirits ever came through to the wrong person, but I never reached him. Still, I'm grateful. That night was the first time I felt sure—Cooper was finding his way through.

These early signs changed everything. I stopped looking for proof and started trusting the quiet ways love finds its way back to us.

For some people, those quiet ways appear as ladybugs, butterflies or dragonflies—small, delicate messages that arrive just when they're needed most. For others, it might be feathers, lights that flicker for no reason, or songs that suddenly play at the perfect moment.

For me, it's the birds—the Yellow Wattlebird, the little brown bird, and Bunjil soaring high above. Each visit feels like love finding a way to say, "I'm still here."

The signs come—through wings, whispers, or wonder—they remind us that love doesn't disappear. It simply changes form.

Chapter 35
The Messages Continue

Four months after Cooper died, I was in deep despair—crying constantly, lost in exhaustion and grief. Our Chiropractor gently suggested Reiki, saying my energy was stuck and that I needed to shift it. I didn't know what to expect, but I went.

When I arrived at my first session, I couldn't even say my name. The healer's kindness was overwhelming. She helped shift something heavy that I hadn't been able to move alone.

The healer explained that Cooper's energy and mine were intertwined—neither of us could move forward.
She said he was holding close, wanting to help Ash, but couldn't while we were still so tightly connected.
Then she paused and asked,
"You have another son?"
I said yes.
"And your daughter?" she continued.
I told her I didn't have a daughter.

She smiled softly.
"Yes, you do—one who has already crossed over. She was waiting for Cooper."

I froze.
Cooper was a twin. I'd lost the twin early in the pregnancy, before 12 weeks. We returned to the hospital the next day for a curette, and the

scan revealed that Cooper was still there—I had lost one baby, but didn't know it was a girl.

The healer said Cooper had known her spirit from a young age. "The pull was too strong," she said. "He had to go to her."

I left shaken—but strangely peaceful.

I continued regularly for some time, finding the experience provided reprieve—especially receiving messages about Cooper and my spirit guides. The difference was so profound that Deane, Ash, my sister, and my mum have all gone. Each of us experienced something unique.

I can't fully explain the depth of those sessions—only that they changed me. They saved me.
Everyone could see the darkness beginning to lift.

A few weeks later, when my sister went, she was told that Cooper hadn't crossed over—that he was still waiting.

Later, at a reading with a medium, she heard something different: Cooper was staying close because he had a message to deliver. We all knew who that message was for—Ash.

When Ash went for his own reading, he didn't tell the medium who he was. The session was meant to last an hour—it went for two and a half. The medium cried the entire time as Cooper came through, full of emotion and apology.

He asked for Ashton's forgiveness. He said he was sorry he left, sorry that Ash was there, but grateful too—that his brother was with him in those final moments. He said he loved him, and that he was proud.

When Ash came home, he said quietly,
"I got more out of that than any psychologist session."

That reading changed something in all of us.
It confirmed what we already felt—that Cooper's energy was strong, his love undiminished, his presence unmistakable.

I continued with Reiki and other forms of healing—sound healing, guided meditation, and energy work.
Each time, Cooper came through.

During one meditation, a young woman with developing psychic abilities said,
"You're surrounded by love. Your son is trying to heal your heart."

At another, a lady said,

"A boy is here with a mother bear. They're standing in a forest. The child makes a 'C' shape from his heart and places it on yours."

I couldn't speak—only cry.
Every time, the message was the same: Cooper's spirit is strong; his love is unbreakable.

I've had four readings—in April, May, August and on his birthday – 5th December, all in the same year Cooper died. Each one was profound. The last brought me to tears when the medium said, "He would hug you a million times over if he could."

I always had to insist Cooper gave me a hug—he'd lean in, barely touching, letting me do the work. It drove me crazy, and he knew it.

Beth once asked him about it, and he'd laughed, saying,

"Treat them mean, keep them keen."
She told him, "It's your mum, not a girlfriend!"
Those words broke and healed me all at once.

───

There have been times when I've felt Cooper close in ways I can't explain. One day, while driving alone to my parents' place in regional Victoria, I was talking out loud to him about my worries.
Suddenly, my car's cruise control braked sharply—on its own, the speed dropping instantly, with no other cars around. It had never done that before and hasn't since. In that instant, I felt him. It was as if he was saying, *That's not right, Mum. You don't need to worry about that.*

───

Even Deane, once a sceptic, now sees the signs.
We've all become believers.

Birds appear in strange places. In my sister's backyard we once had a bird sit on the fence all day, following us from back to front as we moved through the house—as if Cooper was making sure we were okay. The bird flew off once we drove off.

───

There's talk about a veil between this world and the next. I believe it's thinner than we think.
Healers have told me that Ash has the ability to connect with Cooper too, though he doesn't yet know how to access it. Sometimes he

wakes at 3a.m.—the same hour I do—with sudden clarity about a decision or a question. I like to think that's Cooper helping him.
In one sound-healing session, I felt an overwhelming warmth and heard a voice say,
"I've got him."
I realised it was my grandfather—Pa—letting me know Cooper was safe, held, and loved. When I told the healer, she smiled softly and said,
"They've both been standing behind you since you walked in."

~

I've only had two dreams where Cooper felt truly present—so vivid and real. In one, I was speaking into a piece of paper like it was a phone, and I could hear him perfectly. It felt so ordinary and extraordinary at once.

He told me the wording on the monument wasn't balanced—and he was right. It's only his name for now, though one day Deane and I will be added too.
When I woke, I cried—not from sadness, but from closeness. Those dreams are rare gifts.

Writing this now, I realise how much I wish I'd recorded every sign from the beginning.
The little things fade too easily. So, if you are grieving, write. Don't worry about perfection—just capture the memories. You'll be grateful later.

~

These experiences—the healings, the signs, the dreams—might

sound unbelievable to some, but to me they are proof of something sacred: love doesn't vanish. It changes form. It finds new ways to reach us.

Cooper's energy is still here—playful, protective, persistent. When I feel that sudden warmth, hear a song, or see a bird hover a moment too long, I smile, because I know, he's saying,
"I'm here, Mum."

Healing isn't about letting go.
It's about learning to listen differently—
to the quiet, unseen ways love still speaks.

Chapter 36
What Grief Taught Me

There's so much advice out there about grief—especially online. Words of comfort, encouragement, and so-called wisdom about how to move forward.

But the reality is, for many of us—especially mothers—we don't want to move on.
We live with our grief.
Not because we're stuck, but because we loved deeply.

Grief, for us, is love with nowhere to go.

In a world that values "getting better" and "being strong," that can be hard to explain. Society wants tidy endings—resolution, smiles and healing. But the kind of loss we've experienced doesn't work that way. When you lose a child, you don't return to who you were before. You learn to live around the absence. You learn to carry it.

I used to say the things people say: *They'd want you to live. You'll be okay. Time heals.*
I know those words came from love—from a desire to comfort—but now I understand how they miss the mark. It's not that they're wrong. It's that they're incomplete.

When someone is grieving, they don't need advice. They don't need fixing. They need to be seen, held, remembered. They need someone willing to sit beside their pain, without trying to make it disappear.

Before Cooper died, I didn't know how to do that.
Now I do. Losing a child isn't just losing a person—it's losing a future. A piece of your identity. A love that was supposed to last a lifetime. It's losing a part of yourself you can never get back.

So now, when I think about grief, I think less about "getting through it" and more about honouring it. About giving it the space it deserves. This isn't a lesson I wanted to learn. But grief has been a relentless teacher. It's taught me that love doesn't end. It doesn't fade. And it doesn't need to be hidden to make others more comfortable.

If you're grieving, you're not broken. You're human.

And if you know someone who is grieving—say their loved one's name. Don't be afraid of their sadness. Be present in it. We don't move on. We move with it.
Because love like this never leaves.

CHAPTER 37
Who Am I Now?

When I wrote the chapter *What I Was, and What I Am,* I was still trying to make sense of who had survived—the version of me left standing when the world fell apart.

Time has passed since then, and I am starting to see things differently. This isn't about what was taken, but what has quietly grown in the space that remains.
It's about how we keep changing, even when we don't notice—how grief reshapes us, but love still finds its way through.

When you reach the end of a story like this, it's almost expected there will be reflection—a sense of what's been learned, of how you've somehow become a better person.

It makes me smile, because I know I'm not "better."
But I am *different*.

～

I see it more clearly in Ash.
He's stepping into that chapter of life you're meant to reach at 18—starting a new job, out and about all the time, connecting with friends, going to the gym. Living his life.
Some nights he's home for dinner, sometimes he's not.

There's an openness to his days again—a sense that life might still hold something good. I remember Cooper reaching this time in his life. For Ash, it was put on hold.

It's nice to see this transition now. It came later than it should have—almost two years delayed—but I know the closeness we built during those long months at home will always stay.

The endless afternoons after school, or the days he'd finish an early shift and be home by midday—that time together mattered more than either of us realised in the moment. It shaped him. It held me. And it gave us something solid to stand on as life slowly began to move again.

Beth still honours her love for Cooper; she never wavers in that.

She's met someone new and is starting to open her heart again—apprehensive, but willing. She's studying, about to finish her qualifications.

She never planned to study—her whole world had been built around a future with Cooper, being his wife and the mother of his children.

Now she sees her studies, her newfound confidence, and her focus on herself first and foremost as a gift from Cooper. A quiet nudge forward. A reminder that her story didn't end the day his did.

And even as she steps into new chapters—love, learning, living again—she carries him with her. Not as a shadow, but as a presence that gently walks beside her, giving her the courage to choose a future she never imagined she'd have to face alone.

Deane has found his wings.
He's started to soar—just as a colleague once said he would.

He's good at what he does, still the kind and thoughtful man he's always been. He's on the countdown to early retirement now. Don't get me wrong—work is tiring, and he thinks about Cooper every single day. But he's found his rhythm again.

And with each step, each day, each small return to himself, I see a man learning to live with a broken heart that still beats with love.

And then I think about me.
What's changed?

I still cry.
I still ache.
But I also live differently now.
I love slower.
I notice more.

Cooper changed who I am—
and I'm learning to live in that new skin.

Each of us has found our own way to survive and to honour Cooper.
No right way.

No wrong way.
Just *our* way.

As time moves on, I see more clearly how love continues to find us—through signs, synchronicities, and moments that remind me Cooper is still here, guiding us forward.

I've shared our story—not because it has an ending, but because it keeps unfolding.

Every day brings a new wave, a new reminder of how love continues.

This book began as a scream in the dark, and ends as a whisper of light—for Cooper, for all of us.

CHAPTER 38
Little Brown Bird

It only recently dawned on me…it's always been about the bird.

In the early days after Coop died, Beth sent me a video—a small, precious moment from Phillip Island.
In it, Coop is playfully mocking our love of birdwatching. With his best David Attenborough impression, he says, *"Look at these birds, so rare, only found at Phillip Island!"* then he laughs and Beth joins in the laughter.

It makes me smile every time I watch it, and I'm so grateful Beth shared it with me. It's a reminder of his humour, his voice, and his joy.

Not long after that, a bird call started visiting me every morning.
A Yellow Wattlebird—its song sounded like it was saying, *"Get up, get up."*
Like a message from beyond.
For months it came, calling me out of bed, reminding me to keep going.
Then came the little brown bird.

Every day it would appear.
Sometimes when I opened the curtains at the front of the house, sometimes at the back door, often on the woodshed roof.
Other times, if I hadn't seen it, I'd wonder where it was—and like magic, it would appear.

It followed me quietly, gently, hopping along fences, flitting across the garden, unconcerned by the dogs or my presence.
Just...there.

That's when I realised—the bird had always been with me. Watching. Comforting.
A companion on this path I never asked to walk.

This is how the name of the business came about—*Little Brown Bird*.
It felt like the only name that made sense.

I asked a friend to read my children's book, *Do You Look at the Sky?*, to her granddaughter, just to hear how it sounded aloud.

I'd read that stories sometimes change when spoken—that they come alive in unexpected ways. To my delight, it was exactly how I had imagined it. My friend, an Early Years teacher, said the rhythm and flow felt natural and warm.

That night, as I was reflecting on whether *Little Brown Bird* was truly the right name for my business, I received a sign. My friend messaged me a photo—her granddaughter had made a collage after our visit.

Now, I need to say—there was no bird in my story, and I hadn't mentioned the business name idea at all. But her granddaughter had titled the collage *Little Brown Bird*.

You can imagine how my heart skipped a beat.
Literally, as I was questioning my decision, that message appeared—and *Little Brown Bird* was born.

The name also connects to Bunjil, the creator—a presence I deeply respect. When Bunjil circles above us, it is an experience that feels powerful and sacred.

Little Brown Bird gives me a quiet strength.
A small, steady guide.
A comfort.
A symbol of something greater.

As I share this story with people, it's remarkable how many have their own stories about a bird.
Many call it a *spirit bird*, drawn from the depth of their experience. There's often an instant connection—a quiet knowing that their loved one is reaching out with tenderness and presence.

But imagine if these birds could speak.
If they could whisper all the things we long to hear—all the words left unsaid.
Oh, what a gift that would be.

Instead, we find comfort in their presence—knowing, hoping, trusting that this small, fragile sign carries far more than we can ever see.

Once you lose someone you love, you never look at birds the same way again.
And some of the stories I've heard are nothing short of miraculous.

Sometimes love has feathers.
It perches quietly nearby, reminding us that we are never truly alone.

Chapter 39
Legacy: Love That Refuses to Disappear

I was telling someone about my children's picture book and how important it is to me—how it gives Cooper's name purpose, how it brings something gentle and helpful out of something so unbearably painful.

Writing *Do You Look at the Sky?* helps children and families navigate grief, but it also helps me. It allows me to keep saying his name. It allows his life to continue touching others. It ensures he isn't forgotten.

The person I was speaking to said something that stayed with me: "Legacy and tributes are essential in grief. They help us understand, honour, and carry the love."

That sentence sank deep. It made me realise that for so many of us, creating legacy is how we survive. It's how we find even the smallest piece of meaning in something that feels completely senseless.

Because if we have to live with this pain—and of course, we don't get a choice—then we will live with purpose. We will live with our child at the centre of the decisions we make, the kindness we offer, the courage we find, and the people we eventually become.

We will make sure the world knows how deeply our child is loved. We will make sure people understand the size of the hole that was

left behind.
We will speak their name, over and over again, even when others stop saying it.

There will never be enough time to say their name as often as our heart needs to hear it—so we find ways to keep saying it, keep sharing it, keep weaving it into the world.

Legacy is not about letting go. It's about holding on—with love, with intention, with honour.
It brings a tiny sense of purpose to something that still doesn't make sense. It gives our love somewhere to go.

Legacy doesn't have to be big. Some people think legacy means a foundation, a scholarship, a building with a plaque. But sometimes, it's written quietly into the heart, woven into who we become, or carried in a small symbol only we understand.

For others it may be a tattoo. I never knew how personal a tattoo could be. In the past, I might have asked someone if their tattoo had meaning—but now I know not to be so intrusive. That simple question might break someone.

What I've also learned is that for some, being visible offers an opportunity to boast about your loved one. I've learned this through Ashton and the way he shares about his brother whenever he can.

Ash has a wave tattoo—signifying him and his brother, while also representing the ocean and our love of Phillip Island.

He has Cooper's full name and date of birth. Simple. Fine line. Yet together, they hold the deepest meaning.

I love that he designed this himself and that it sits proudly on his inner forearm. The waves also carry a hidden message—the ebb and flow of grief.

When I got my tattoo, Beth and I went together.

Beth had Cooper's handwriting etched on the outside of her forearm, so whenever she lifts her arm, everyone can see it. His writing was from a card he'd sent, expressing his love, with the words—*"through thick and thin."* Every time I think of Beth doing that, I smile. How beautiful that Coop made a permanent mark on her arm, and on her heart.

I have an infinity ring—to represent my endless love for Cooper—with his name and a Yellow Wattlebird in flight. That's the bird from his birdwatching video, the one that still visits our garden at home and at the Island. It was also that bird's call that told me, *"Get up, get up!"* in my early days of grief.

These visible symbols—etched, worn, or carried—keep our love close. They remind us that legacy doesn't only live in grand gestures, but in the quiet ways we choose to keep them with us.

Legacy can be:

- Writing their name in the sand at the beach.
- Planting a tree in their honour.
- Wearing their birth stone.
- Lighting a candle every birthday.
- Speaking about them in the present tense.
- Donating to a cause they cared about.
- Carrying on a tradition they loved.
- Sharing their story, even when your voice shakes.

- Living your life the way they would be proud of.

Legacy can simply be love in action.
And it can change over time.

In the early days, legacy might be survival—getting out of bed, breathing through another day. That, in itself, honours them.

Later, it may become writing, art, advocacy, helping others, or creating something in their memory.

And sometimes, legacy is quiet.
It's private moments no one else sees.
It's whispering *I love you* into the night.
It's carrying them forward in every step you take.

Most importantly...

There is no right or wrong way to honour your child.
It doesn't have to be public.
It doesn't have to be perfect.
It doesn't have to make sense to anyone else.
It just has to connect your heart to the love that still lives inside you.

Because the love does not end—and legacy is simply that love continuing its journey in the world.

However you choose to remember them, speak of them, or build in their honour...
that is legacy.

That is love that refuses to disappear.
And that love—their love—will always matter.

This book and the children's book—*Do You Look at the Sky?*—is Cooper's legacy.
But it's also mine.
Because legacy isn't just about the person who's gone.
It's also about who we become in the loving that remains.

Chapter 40
Until We Meet Again

I always thought I'd live until my nineties.
Longevity runs in my family—even if our bodies need a few repairs along the way (hence the knee replacement).

That was the plan.
No intention of going anywhere early.

But when your child dies, your perspective changes.

If I live to ninety, I will have lived forty years without Coop. How is that even possible?
I can't imagine it.
I don't want to imagine it.

~

I'd never really thought about death before. I wasn't afraid of it—I just never spent much time contemplating it.

Now, I know there will be no fear, no hesitation. Not for me, and not for many members of our family. Because Cooper will be there to meet us.

His big grin.
That sassy smirk.
His long grey jacket, pink shirt, RM Williams boots.

Business card in his pocket.
Shades on.
Full of love—his heart exploding—ready, waiting for us at the front of the line. (He may have nudged or talked his way through to the front—always the charmer—ready to give us the VIP treatment.)

For him, I'm sure it will have felt like five minutes apart.
For us, it will have felt like a lifetime.

∼

Finally together again.
We'll look over our family.
I won't need to fill him in on anything—he'll already know.
He's been with us all the way along.
So I know, as I say this out aloud, he is listening:

Coop,
I am proud of you.
Thank you for helping my hand race across the page with such vigour.
Thank you for placing the courage in front of me, so I could find it—I might not have found it on my own.
I'm proud to be your mum.
I'm proud that together, we can help others find a way to navigate their grief.
Every day, I wish for a different ending.
Every day I look for you.
I love you, and I miss you—with all my being.

Love always,
Mum x

∼

And until that day comes, I'll keep writing, keep loving, and keep saying your name.

Chapter 41
The Shape of Hope

People often ask how I keep going.
The truth is—I don't always know.
There's no magic formula, no grand revelation.
Some days, I barely make it to the end.

But somewhere between the pain and the love, I've found a kind of rhythm—a softer way of breathing through this life I didn't choose.

～

To be honest, some days I cope by pretending Coop is in Brisbane—busy with his job, loving the challenge, meeting new people, and calling Deane to proudly share everything he's achieving.
Calling me early in the morning, eager to connect and tell me what is happening. Always a laugh. Conversations always ending with I love you Coop.

Those moments make life feel bearable.
Even though I know it isn't real, the imagining gives me a few breaths of relief—a soft place to land when the world feels too sharp.

Pretending is possible.
Reality is the part that feels unimaginable.

Grief hasn't left me. It never will.
But it's changed shape.

In the early days, it was chaos—heavy, sharp, consuming.
Every sound, every silence, every morning felt like betrayal.
The world kept spinning, and I wanted to scream: *Stop! Don't you know he's gone?*
But the world doesn't stop.
And neither, somehow, do we.

Now, grief sits differently.
It's quieter, gentler—like a shadow that walks beside me instead of crushing me.
Sometimes it still steals my breath,
but sometimes...it reminds me that love is still here, too.

When I feel the sun on my skin, I think of Cooper.
When the dogs run wild in the yard, I think of Cooper.
When I hear a song that makes my heart ache, I think of Cooper.
But now I can smile *as well as cry.*
That's how I know I'm beginning to heal.
Not healed—just healing.

The truth is, healing isn't about moving on.
It's about *moving with.*
With the love.
With the pain.
With the memories that built you and the heartbreak that reshaped you.

It's all the same thing now—woven together, inseparable.

When people say, "He'd want you to be happy."
I know they mean well, but I don't think happiness is the goal.
Peace is.
Connection is.
Love is.
To still feel him in small, sacred ways—that's all I now have.

And maybe that's what it means—*from pain to purpose.*
Not a neat transformation, not a moment of arrival, but a slow unfolding. Purpose isn't found in moving on. It's in choosing, again and again, to let love guide the way through the ache.

That's what keeps me here—writing, remembering, rebuilding. Not because the pain is gone, but because the love is still so strong. Writing has given me purpose again.

It's helped me speak his name over and over—
and through that, I've realised:
Cooper isn't just in the past.
He's in everything I create now.
Every word, every sentence, every act of love.
He's threaded through all of it.

Hope isn't loud. It doesn't arrive with fireworks or grand gestures.
It's quiet—
like a little brown bird sitting on the fence.
It's the whisper in the wind that says, *Keep going, Mum.*
It's the moment I laugh and don't feel guilty for it.
It's Ashton's smile when he talks about his brother.
It's the peace in knowing that love—real, enduring love—never ends.

That's the shape of hope.
It doesn't erase the ache,

but it reminds me that my story—*our* story—isn't over.

Because every time I speak his name,
every time I write,
every time I love...
Cooper feels closer.
And sometimes, that is the only thing holding me together.

Final Note
When the Words Stop

I keep coming back here to write more. For weeks I wrote every day, and I felt like I was finding a little healing in the rhythm of it. But now everything is in its final stages. The manuscript is with the editor, and all I can do is wait to see whether what I've written has any merit. And so here I am again—just me and my grief.

For the first time in a long time, it's only me and the weight on my chest.

Yesterday I sat on the couch and simply could not move. I binged some mindless show—something I never do. I gave myself tiny tasks: wash the plant leaves, water the garden. But moving felt impossible. My body was heavy. My heart heavier.

I reached out to a couple of people, just a simple, "Hey, not having a great day today."
They sent back love hearts and kind words—and I appreciated them—but the truth is everyone else is living their lives, and I am stuck.

Stuck in missing Coop.
Stuck in grief.
Stuck in a body that sometimes won't move.

When Deane and Ashton came home, I pretended I'd been busy all day.

They wouldn't know whether I had cleaned, gardened, worked hard, or done nothing at all.
They don't mind either way—they only care when the weight becomes too heavy.

But a whole day on the couch...a whole day doing nothing...that is the part people don't see.

And then the thoughts come:
What is the point?
Why are we here?
Why put us on this earth only to take our children from us?
Why my beautiful boy?
Why Coop?

This morning the sun came up, the birds were chirping, and I just lay there thinking...
It's the same again today.
And relief washed over me that I didn't have to face the world.

The thought of returning to work terrifies me.
I used to be the person who arrived early, stayed late, answered every call, always available, always doing.
I don't even know who I am anymore.
I don't know who I want to be.

All I know is that I cannot change this reality.

So, I wanted to write this—for the mother reading who feels helpless.
If this is how you feel, it is normal.
It comes without warning.
It sneaks up when you think you're coping.

Maybe it's because Christmas is coming.
Maybe it's because everyone around me is making plans like life is ordinary.

Maybe it's because Coop's birthday is just weeks away, and I have to survive another one without him.

The weight of heartbreak is enormous.
And I'm sorry to those around me who see my sorrow leak through, even when I think I'm hiding it.

You can't know.
No one can know.
Everyone's grief is personal.

So let me say this plainly:
There is no packing grief neatly into a box.
It is messy.
It is relentless.
It is heartbreaking.
It is the rollercoaster no mother wants a ticket for—moments of functioning, followed by collapsing, followed by trying again.
Falling apart and putting yourself back together every single day is exhausting.

Take care, dear reader.
Others can love you, support you, sit beside you—but they cannot fix this.
You simply find small ways to be kind to yourself.
Small ways to honour your child.
Small ways to keep loving them in this new, impossible world.

I wanted to share this because I never want anyone in grief to think I've figured it all out.
I want to be real and honest about the days that break you.

So now this is really the end of the written story, I know there is no real ending—not to grief, not to love, not to the bond I carry with Cooper.

What comes next is not on these pages—it's in the living. In the choices we make, the support we accept, the honesty we allow, and the strength we find on the days we least expect it.

I don't have all the answers, and I never will, but I do know this: we keep going because we must, and we carry our children with us in every step. This is not an ending. It's simply where I close the book—and where we each continue with our own story, in our own time, in our own way.

Thank You

To everyone who has ever loved and lost—
Thank you for finding your way to these pages. I hope something here helped you feel less alone, more seen, and reminded you that love never leaves us. We just learn new ways to listen for it.

To everyone who has walked beside me—
Thank you.

To the compassionate professionals—
Our GP, chiropractor, psychologists, healers, and everyone who helped us find light—
thank you for giving us tools to rebuild when life felt unrepairable.

To support groups—
The mothers and families of Connecting Mothers in Grief and The Compassionate Friends of Victoria—you gave me understanding when no one else could.
You helped me feel seen, normal, and never alone.

To those who spoke Cooper's name—
who remember him,
who share stories and laughter and tears—
you have no idea how much that meant,
and still means.

To our dear friends—
Thank you for your patience, your honesty, and your unwavering love.
You reminded me that connection can exist even in the darkest spaces.

To our family—
My parents and my in-laws, my sister, and our extended family—
your strength and compassion made survival possible.
You took on the hard things so I could simply breathe.

To my nieces and nephews—
Thank you for loving Cooper in your own beautiful ways,
for the smiles, the memories, the gentle ways you keep his name alive.
Your innocence, your kindness, and the way you continue to include
him reminds me that love echoes through every generation.
You each hold a piece of him,
and in doing so, you help hold me too.

To Beth—
Thank you for loving Cooper so completely,
and for continuing to love me.
You will always be part of our family,
always part of his story.

To Deane, my rock—
Your love is strong.
I know you've wanted to fix me, even though you know that what
was broken can never be fully repaired.
We are strong—we always have been.
The saying we used to share,
"What doesn't kill you makes you stronger,"
this nearly did.
Thank heavens we had each other.
This road will never end, but at least we will walk it hand in hand.

To my beautiful Ashton—
You have carried more than any young man should ever have to.
Your courage, your humour, your love—
they inspire me every day.

You and Cooper are, and always will be, my greatest teachers.

And to Cooper—
My boy, my heart, my light.
You are in every page of this book, every breath I take, every word I write.
Thank you for continuing to find ways to reach me,
for giving me purpose when I had none,
for reminding me that love never ends.

This book exists because of love—
the love that holds us,
the love that heals us,
the love that continues.

**Written in loving memory of
Cooper Reid—Forever 25.
Forever loved, forever remembered, forever missed.**

Author's Note

When I first started writing, I didn't set out to write a book—I simply needed somewhere for my love, my pain, and my memories to go.

Each word became a bridge between the world I knew and the world I now live in.

This book is not a guide. It's not a lesson. It's simply one mother's truth—raw, imperfect, and real.
If it helps even one person feel understood, seen, or a little less alone in their grief, then it has done its job.

Grief doesn't end, but neither does love.
And somewhere between the two—in the space of remembrance, storytelling, and connection—we find a way to live again.

Thank you for reading, for bearing witness, and for holding space for Cooper's story.
My hope is that his light, and the love that shaped these pages, continues to ripple outward—
softly, quietly, endlessly.

With love and gratitude,

Vicki Reid

About the Author

Vicki Reid is a devoted mother, wife, and writer from the South Eastern suburbs of Melbourne in Victoria, Australia.
A lifelong educator and advocate for the rights of children and emotional wellbeing, Vicki has spent her career helping others find their voice—a gift she now uses to honour the memory of her son, Cooper.

Following Cooper's sudden death in 2024, writing became her way to survive—a way to give shape to love, loss, and everything in between.
Her heartfelt reflections, first shared privately in journals and letters, grew into this deeply personal memoir of grief, resilience, and connection.

Vicki is also the author of *Do You Look at the Sky?*, a children's picture book that helps families gently explore grief, love, and remembrance together.

When she's not writing, Vicki finds peace in the garden, walking along the beach at Phillip Island, and spending time with her husband, Deane, and their son, Ashton.
Through her words and work, she continues to keep Cooper's name, spirit, and legacy alive—reminding others that love never ends.

Little Brown Bird
www.littlebrownbird.com.au

Do You Look at the Sky?

Do You Look at the Sky? is a heartfelt story for children who love someone they never got to meet, yet carry in their hearts through the stories their family shares.

How can you love someone you don't know? Somehow...you just do. You imagine their smile, wonder who they were, and feel them in the quiet moments when you look up at the sky.

A warm, tender book about a love that lingers, memories that stay, and the gentle magic of looking up.

www.ingramcontent.com/pod-product-compliance
Lightning Source LLC
Chambersburg PA
CBHW021100080526
44587CB00010B/322